UNDERSTANDING NEUROPSYCHOLOGY

Basic Psychology

UNDERSTANDING
NEUROPSYCHOLOGY

J. Graham Beaumont

Basil Blackwell

First published 1988

Basil Blackwell Ltd
108 Cowley Road, Oxford, OX4 1JF, UK

Basil Blackwell Inc.
432 Park Avenue South, Suite 1503
New York, NY 10016, USA

BRITISH LIBRARY CATALOGUING IN PUBLICATION DATA

Beaumont, J. Graham
  Understanding neuropsychology.
  1. Neuropsychology
  I. Title
  152   QP360

  ISBN 0–631–15719–0
  ISBN 0–631–15721–2 Pbk

LIBRARY OF CONGRESS CATALOGING IN PUBLICATION DATA

Beaumont, J. Graham
  Understanding neuropsychology.
  (Basic psychology)
  Bibliography: p.
  Includes index.
  1. Neuropsychology.   I. Title.   II. Series:
Basic psychology (Oxford, Oxfordshire) [DNLM:
1. Neuropsychology.   WL 103 B379u]
QP360.B417   1987   612'.8   87–11562
ISBN 0–631–15719–0
ISBN 0–361–15721–2 (pbk.)

Typeset in 10 on 12 pt Palatino
by Columns
Printed in Great Britain by Page Bros (Norwich) Ltd

Contents

Series Preface

Psychology is a relatively new science which has already made notable achievements; yet its methods are constantly being questioned and redefined. This book is one of a series of introductory psychology texts, designed to convey the fast-moving and relevant nature of contemporary research while at the same time encouraging the reader to develop a critical perspective on the methodology and data presented. The format of the books is intended to aid such independent inquiry, as is shown in particular by the boxes at the end of each chapter that concentrate on individual studies as 'worked examples'.

The books in the Basic Psychology series should be accessible to those who have no previous knowledge of the discipline. *Understanding Neuropsychology* can profitably be used by students on their own without a teacher, but resources aimed at group work, for example as part of social work or teacher training courses, are also included: a further reading section, discussion points and practical exercises follow each chapter.

Peter K. Smith

Author's Preface

This book, together with its companions in the series, grew out of a project which was originally designed to create a single textbook introducing psychology. As the project developed it became clear that our aims could best be realized by a number of integrated texts which could each stand alone as representing one perspective on human behaviour and mental life. This book is, in part, the result.

We began this project with the belief that two main aims were not incompatible: the provision of a general text which would be appropriate for students studying 'A' level Psychology in schools and colleges and the creation of an introductory text which would be accessible to the general, but serious, reader who wished to explore the contemporary discipline of psychology. The content of the text therefore follows very closely the syllabus for the Joint Matriculation Board examination in Psychology (Advanced), and it is no accident that the authors of the volumes have been associated with the JMB 'A' level examinations in various capacities. However, it so happens that the JMB 'A' level syllabus is particularly broad and comprehensive in its coverage of modern psychology. This syllabus is modelled very closely on the typical content of a first-year undergraduate course in psychology – certainly in its breadth if not its depth. As a result it provides an excellent starting point for any student beginning their exploration of psychology, irrespective of their context of study.

With the decision to divide the original text into a series of modules, it was obvious that one of the modules should be concerned with the biological background within which behaviour occurs. One quarter of the JMB syllabus is entitled 'Biological bases of behaviour', and the content of this text closely follows that section. It is, in itself, divided into four chapters. The first provides a general introduction to the structure and function of the nervous system. The gross neuroanatomy of the system is described, as are the methods used by psychologists to investigate the operation of the nervous system. The general principles of neural and hormonal transmission are discussed, including neurons, synapses and transmitter substances. The particular role played by hormones is also explained.

The second chapter deals with information processing in the nervous system by examining the mechanisms of sensation and perception in the visual and auditory systems. For each system, its general structure is described, followed by an account of how sensory information is encoded within the system. Perception is then presented as a modification of the sensory information by further processing.

The cortex of the brain is the subject of the third chapter. Again, its structure is described and its functions presented by the discussion of two particular topics: speech and language, and the control of movement. The principles of cortical function are explained by showing the psychological systems which operate and how these relate to the anatomy of the brain by considering the effects of damage to selected areas. The chapter concludes with a discussion of lateral asymmetry in the brain and the debate concerning the degree of localization of function. The work of clinical neuropsychologists is illustrated and certain philosophical issues about the relationship between brain and mind are introduced.

The final chapter addresses the functions of the subcortical forebrain. These functions are discussed under the topics of emotion, arousal and awareness and motivation. Not only are the systems which generate emotional experience discussed, together with the theories about their operation, but also the origins and control of aggression, and the current status of psychosurgery. 'Arousal and awareness' provides an opportunity to discuss sleep and the altered states of consciousness of hypnosis, meditation and anaesthesia, as well as the study of the electrical activity of the brain. Needs, drives and reward are the elementary aspects of motivation presented in the final section, together with hunger and thirst and sexual activity, and the brain mechanisms which provide the human ability to learn.

The emphasis of the book is as much upon the applications and relevance of psychological science as upon the formal knowledge and concepts which are at the heart of the science. There is an attempt to describe what is happening on the frontiers of research, as well as to present the classical findings and well established phenomena which are the core of psychological knowledge. Methods are introduced and discussed, and there is an attempt to develop a questioning, critical approach to the subject and its literature.

For this reason, each chapter contains not only the main text, but also two examples of recent studies from the psychological literature which are relevant to the content of the chapter. The design of the research, the methods used in the investigation and the analysis and interpretation of the results are all presented in some detail. There is a critical appraisal of the research and the significance of the findings is set in the psychological context. Each chapter also contains suggestions for simple practical experiments which can be carried out without specialized facilities. There are suggestions for discussion and essay topics for those wishing to pursue their study in a more formal context, as well as a guide to further reading. The chapters are quite substantially referenced for an introductory text.

Why *Understanding Neuropsychology* rather than, say, 'Understanding the Biological Bases of Behaviour'? The simplest answer is that the first title seems more accurately to represent the approach to psychology being adopted within this book. It takes the view that one way to understand how and why humans behave as they do is to try to understand what the brain is doing, and what influence it has upon the activity it is involved in generating. This is really more specific than considering all the biological influences which affect behaviour: ecological, genetic, biochemical and sociobiological, in addition to those concerned with the nervous system. The neurosciences have been an area of particularly spectacular development over the past couple of decades, and this has been reflected in the growing importance of neuropsychology within psychology. The book seeks to introduce the neuroscience perspective to psychology and to demonstrate that this is a valuable approach to gaining an insight into the workings of the human mind.

As a neuropsychology text, this book perhaps contains a little more about sensation and perception than might have been anticipated. It nevertheless contains coverage of the two main approaches to neuropsychology: the study of normal humans in the laboratory and brain-damaged patients in the clinic to investigate the higher cortical functions; and the use of animal experiments to demonstrate the processes involved at the subcortical level of function. The emphasis is, however, clearly upon the human studies, although one of the strengths of the book should be the way in which it brings together these two approaches, too often regarded as separate types of neuropsychology.

The book therefore provides a broad and, within the space available, comprehensive introduction to neuropsychology. Taken with its companion volumes it forms part of a general introduction to the subject matter of psychology, the methods which psychologists use and the ways in which psychological knowledge can be applied. It should be invaluable to 'A' level students and others pursuing formal courses in psychology within schools, colleges and Further Education institutions. Even at the introductory level of degree course studies there are students who may well find the kind of approach adopted here to be valuable. In addition it will be useful to those studying psychology as part of other professional education: in the paramedical field, in business and management and in social and biological studies. Finally, I would hope that it would be of sufficient clarity and interest to engage and stimulate the 'lay' reader to find out more of what psychology has to offer.

It will not surprise you that I find psychology a fascinating and engaging subject. One of the delights of studying psychology is that it is such a broad discipline and has links with so many other areas of study. A psychologist can be involved one moment in neurophysiology, at another in computer science, at another in aesthetics and at another in philosophy. All these are involved – even within the field of neuropsychology. Particularly exciting is the challenge of understanding just how the human brain operates and how it gives rise to the rich variety of conscious experience and the amazing flexibility, skill and power of human intellect. If I can only communicate a little of the excitement of this challenge, and encourage others to take up the rewarding study of psychology, then this book will have succeeded.

J. Graham Beaumont
Leicester

1

The Nervous System

The General Structure of the Nervous System

It is important for psychologists to understand the nervous system because it is the principal mechanism by which our perception, thinking and action are achieved. Knowing the structure of the system may give us clues about how these psychological functions are organized. Psychologists are also interested in how changes in the nervous system, caused by damage, disease, or the effects of drugs, are related to changes in behaviour. This is not only in order to extend psychological knowledge, but also to contribute to the treatment and rehabilitation of the brain damaged and mentally ill.

The nervous system is conventionally divided into three parts: the **peripheral nervous system** (PNS) which lies outside the skull and spinal column, the **central nervous system** (CNS) which is the brain and spinal cord inside the skull and spinal column, and the **autonomic nervous system** (ANS). The PNS and CNS are quite distinct, but the ANS is made up of components of both the PNS and ANS and connects to the internal organs of the body.

Peripheral nervous system

The function of the PNS is to gather information and pass it to the CNS, and to pass out information from the CNS to the sites where commands will be carried out.

The structures which gather this information are called **receptors**, and they are distributed around the body. In the skin different types of receptor detect light touch, pain and temperature; pressure, pain and position sense are detected by receptors lying beneath the skin and in deep tissue; and pain can be detected from the internal organs (figure 1.1). Connections are made with the CNS at particular points along the spinal cord. These links from receptors to the CNS form an **afferent** system, because the messages are carried up *to* the brain.

Information is also carried down and *away* from the brain through an

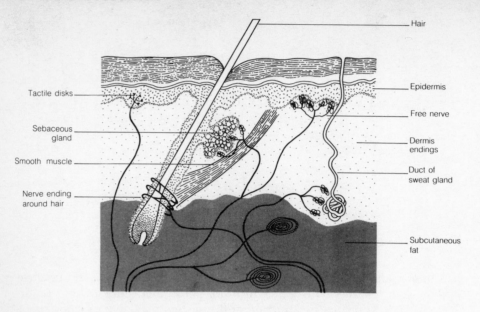

Hair

Epidermis

Free nerve

Dermis
endings

Duct of
sweat gland

Subcutaneous
fat

Tactile disks

Sebaceous
gland

Smooth muscle

Nerve ending
around hair

FIGURE 1.1 *Some examples of receptors lying in and under the skin*

efferent system in the PNS. Links at the spinal cord carry messages to **effectors** which are situated in muscles and glands around the body. The intentions of the CNS can therefore be translated into actions by the operation of muscles, or the release of substances from glands which will alter the operation of bodily processes.

There is one further important element in the PNS. The **cranial nerves** are the only part of the PNS not to link with the spinal cord. They are arranged in 12 pairs and are joined directly to the base of the brain. The cranial nerves deal almost exclusively with the skin and organs of the head and neck, including the mouth, tongue and throat. Sensations from these areas are conducted by the cranial nerves, which also control their movement. Some cranial nerves are purely efferent, some purely afferent, and some perform both functions. Three of the pairs are particularly important to us because they are concerned with **special senses**: pair I, the olfactory nerves serving smell; pair II, the optic nerves serving vision; and pair VIII, the acoustic or auditory nerves serving hearing and the sense of balance (see chapter 2).

One important difference between the PNS and the CNS is that when the PNS is injured it is possible for the damaged nerves to regenerate, establishing new growth and re-forming their connections. This is not possible in the CNS. There is no significant structural recovery from damage to the CNS.

Although the PNS is in reality a very complex system, it is sufficient for us to consider it as a communications link between the spinal cord and the periphery of the body, with the addition of the cranial nerves serving the special senses.

Central nervous system

The CNS is contained within the bony case of the skull and the spinal column. As it is particularly vulnerable to injury, this gives it added protection. It is also surrounded by **cerebrospinal fluid** (CSF) which supplies certain nutrients and also acts to cushion movements transmitted to the system. This fluid is produced under pressure in chambers inside the brain (called the ventricles), and it circulates around the CNS until it is absorbed into the blood supply. When the circulation is obstructed, hydrocephalus or 'water-on-the-brain' may result. Three membranes, the **meninges**, also cover the system, protecting and supporting it. It is these membranes which becomes inflamed in meningitis.

The CNS may be divided up as in figure 1.2 and figure 1.3 which shows a midline section through the head viewed from the side. The principal division is between the brain and the spinal cord.

The **spinal cord** can be considered as a chain of levels, each level relating to one of the vertebrae (bones) of the spinal column. At each level there are two pairs of nerve roots which provide the links to the PNS. The nerves in the PNS which connect to a particular level of the spinal cord supply a clearly defined horizontal band on the surface of the body. By identifying the location of abnormal sensation on the skin, a neurologist can detect the location of disease in the spinal cord (Wiederholt, 1982).

The cord is not merely a pathway for passing messages up and down between the brain and the PNS. Certain simple behaviours are organized within the cord, mainly by means of **reflexes**. In a simple reflex, the sensory information enters from the PNS at one level of the spinal cord, and then links directly by a **reflex arc** to an efferent motor nerve which passes back out to the PNS at the same level of the cord. Some more complex reflexes are organized over several adjacent levels of the spinal cord, but all are accomplished without direct control from higher levels in the brain. The brain can control the speed of reflexes, and how easily they are triggered, but not the details of their operation. Examples of reflexes are the jerk of the knee when the knee-cap is struck with a soft hammer, or the curling up of the toes when the sole of the foot is scratched.

The **brain** may be divided into the cerebrum, and the **cerebellum** ('little brain') (figure 1.2). The cerebellum's main role is to co-ordinate muscular activity in both posture and movement. The position of the body is maintained by sets of muscles working against each other. If they were not properly co-ordinated then stable positions such as standing or sitting could not be maintained, movements would be jerky and inaccurate, and there would be the real danger of bones being broken by muscles. The cerebellum supervises all this activity and ensures that the muscles operate in harmony, all without conscious effort on the individual's part. It is a tribute to the

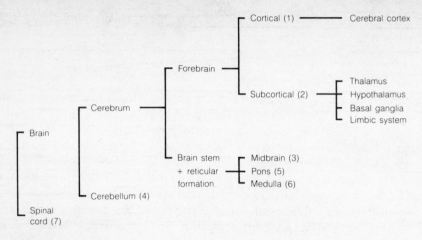

FIGURE 1.2   *The principal divisions of the CNS (numbers refer to the structures labelled in figure 1.3)*

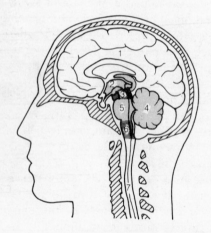

FIGURE 1.3   *The principal divisions of the CNS (see figure 1.2) (From Beaumont, 1983)*

cerebellum that we can not only avoid self-injury, but execute the most fine, delicate and graceful of movements. The cerebellum sits astride the brain stem behind and below the forebrain (figure 1.3). It has direct connections not only with the brain stem but down into the spinal cord and up into the highest levels of the brain.

The **cerebrum** is divided into brain stem and forebrain (figure 1.2). The **brain stem** lies immediately above the spinal cord and includes the **medulla** ('marrow'), the **pons** ('bridge') and the **midbrain** (figure 1.3). One of the main roles of this area is the maintenance of vital functions. Blood pressure is controlled here, as are respiration, salivation and movements of the

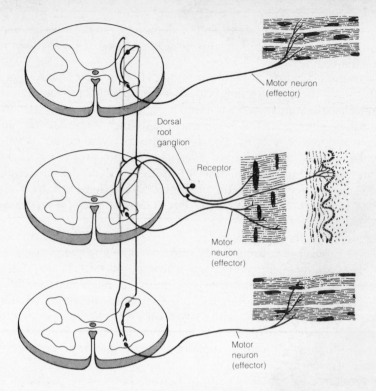

Motor neuron
(effector)

Dorsal
root
ganglion

Receptor

Motor
neuron
(effector)

Motor
neuron
(effector)

FIGURE 1.4 *Reflex arcs in the spinal cord (Amended from an illustration by F. Netter, MD(c). Reproduced by courtesy of Ciba-Geigy PLC Basle. All rights reserved)*

alimentary canal. If you vomit, it is triggered from the brain stem. The cranial nerves enter the CNS at this point, so that information from the special senses is passing through this region. Some forms of visual reflex including blinking, constriction of the pupil and certain eye movements are organized here. The startle reflex, jumping at a sudden noise, also originates here.

An important structure running through the brain stem is the **reticular formation** ('net-like'), which connects with structures in the spinal cord, cerebellum and the higher regions of the brain. In particular the **ascending reticular activating system** (ARAS) receives inputs from afferent sensory pathways as they pass upward, and in turn acts upon higher levels. The result is generalized arousal of the whole forebrain, so maintaining consciousness, wakefulness and attention. The ARAS ensures that the brain is in a state of readiness to receive the specific sensory information as it arrives.

The **forebrain** of the cerebrum can sensibly be divided into its cortical and subcortical parts (figure 1.2). The **subcortical forebrain** is centrally involved in motivation, emotion and states of awareness as well as sensation, motor control and memory. There are three main structures in this region: the thalamus ('inner room'), the hypothalamus ('lower room') which lies below it, and the basal ganglia which is a collection of neural centres deep in the middle of the brain.

All the afferent sensory pathways, and the efferent motor pathways, with the exception of those controlling voluntary purposeful movements, travel to and from the **thalamus**. Although much of the information is then passed on up to the cerebral cortex, it is the thalamus which is the real terminus of the sensory and motor systems. The loop to the cortex no doubt allows more sophisticated control, and probably gives us conscious awareness of sensory and motor events, but the thalamus provides the central registration and control. Sensation received at the thalamus is not localized to a specific perception, but is in terms of a general awareness of touch, temperature, or pain.

Damage to the thalamus may result in tremor (at rest, not during movement), rapid jerky involuntary movements, and poor control over movements. Parkinsonism, which not uncommonly afflicts the elderly, is associated with thalamic tremor, with rigidity in movement, and with a shuffling gait and loss of emotional expression. It is interesting to note that the resting tremor of a patient with Parkinson's disease disappears while an intentional movement, such as drinking from a cup, is made. It reappears as soon as attention is diverted, sometimes with disastrous consequences (Pincus and Tucker, 1978).

The **hypothalamus** contains pairs of neural centres which control eating and drinking, sleeping and waking, sexual behaviour, organization for fight or flight and the rage reaction: functions at the 'animal level' of behaviour. These pairs of centres can be thought of as turning the behaviour 'on' or 'off', although the system is in reality rather more complex. Damage to the centres can cause, for instance, incessant eating leading to gross obesity, or else a total failure to eat.

The hypothalamus also controls the response to reward and punishment, and so plays a part in learning. Experimental animals will work extremely vigorously, on a treadmill or pressing a bar, if this results in parts of the hypothalamus receiving electrical stimulation. It can be inferred that this stimulation gives an experience of 'pleasure' (Rolls, 1979).

The **basal ganglia** are associated with the functions of the thalamus and hypothalamus. Parts of the basal ganglia, together with parts of the cortex, form the **limbic system**, which is specifically concerned with memory and learning, aggression and taming, some aspects of object recognition, and sexual and exploratory behaviour. The limbic system seems to organize these behaviours and control their execution, while the hypothalamus is more concerned with their initiation in relation to the current level of motivation (Dimond, 1980). These and other aspects of the function of the subcortical forebrain will be discussed in chapter 4.

The final division of the brain is the **cortical forebrain**, the **cerebral cortex** ('rind' or 'bark'). This is the structure which provides our most human

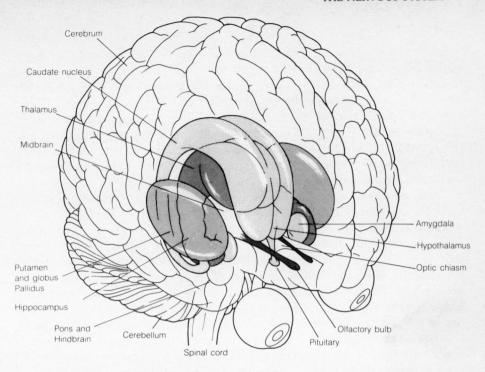

Cerebrum

Caudate nucleus

Thalamus

Midbrain

Putamen
and globus
Pallidus

Hippocampus

Pons and
Hindbrain

Cerebellum

Spinal cord

Amygdala

Hypothalamus

Optic chiasm

Olfactory bulb

Pituitary

FIGURE 1.5   *Structures in the subcortical forebrain (After Nauta and Feirtag, 1979. Copyright © 1979 by Scientific American, Inc. All rights reserved)*

capabilities. It gives us conscious awareness and experience, provides perception, learning and memory, and supports problem solving and intelligent behaviour. It will be discussed more fully in chapter 3.

All structures in the forebrain are paired so that there are *two* thalami, two mirror-image sides to the basal ganglia, and two sides to the cortex. These form two **hemispheres**, on the left and right of the brain, which are relatively independent apart from their interconnection by some special neural pathways (figure 1.5).

It can be useful to think about the CNS in terms of a series of levels from the lowest, the spinal cord, successively through the brain stem and subcortical forebrain, to the highest level of the cerebral cortex. The behaviour which is organized at each level becomes increasing complex, adaptable and sophisticated as we progress up the system. It is interesting that if we consider the system in terms of how recently each part of the system evolved (which is called phylogenetic development) then its evolution follows this same pattern. The structures in the spinal cord are the oldest and the behaviour, which we share with all animals, most primitive. The highest level, the cortex, is most distinctively human in its structure and the behaviour organized there, and is the most recently evolved (Oakley and Plotkin, 1979).

Autonomic nervous system

The ANS is comprised of components in both the central and peripheral nervous systems. The main command centre of the ANS is in the hypothalamus, although it is also under control from the cerebral cortex, and has direct links with the system of hormonal regulation (see below). From the hypothalamus the system passes down through the brain stem, interacting with elements of the reticular activating system, and down into the spinal cord, which it leaves by two branches. These are the sympathetic and parasympathetic branches. They have complementary functions and are organized in different ways.

The **sympathetic** branch leaves the spinal cord from its central region, and forms a series of relay stations which are all interconnected in a chain of **ganglia**. It then travels out to reach blood vessels, sweat glands, muscle fibres in the skin, and organs in the head, neck, thorax, abdomen and pelvis. It tends to have an overall 'blanket' action on all these organs, because the interconnections along the chain of ganglia rapidly spread activity out through the whole sympathetic branch.

The **parasympathetic** branch, by contrast, leaves the CNS by the top and bottom sections of the spinal cord, and also by certain of the cranial nerves, and it runs more directly to the various target organs. These are organs in the head as well as the main internal organs. There are, however, *no* connections to blood vessels, to sweat glands, or to the muscle of the skin, except in special cases.

The functions of the two branches are complementary, and in general the sympathetic branch promotes activation for rapid and energetic response, while the parasympathetic branch produces de-activation for relaxation and the conservation of bodily resources. Sympathetic activation is often described as for 'fight and flight', and produces the kind of bodily changes you experience after a sudden fright or when you are all 'keyed up'. Parasympathetic activity is what you experience when dozing comfortably in an armchair after a satisfying meal.

Some of the specific effects of the two branches on target organs are shown in table 1.1. The general level of bodily arousal is roughly a function of the predominance of one or the other branch, but the two branches can be more or less active together. Before an examination you may well experience sweating and pounding of the heart (sympathetic), but you may also feel the need to keep going to the toilet (parasympathetic). There are also behaviours in which the two branches need to co-operate: in sexual intercourse the male genitals must maintain erection (parasympathetic), but then at the appropriate moment produce ejaculation (sympathetic). So you will see that although it is generally true that the sympathetic and parasympathetic branches of the ANS have opposing and complementary effects, their operation is not just a simple see-saw.

Chapter 4 deals further with the functions of the ANS and how they can be measured.

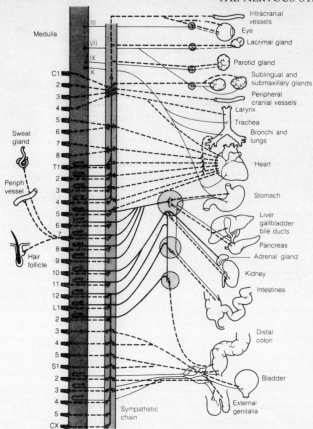

FIGURE 1.6 *The sympathetic and parasympathetic branches of the ANS (Amended from an illustration by F. Netter, MD(c). Reproduced by courtesy of Ciba-Geigy PLC Basle. All rights reserved)*

TABLE 1.1 *Some effects of the sympathetic and parasympathetic branches of the ANS on certain target organs*

Organ	Sympathetic	Parasympathetic
Heart	speeds	slows
Peripheral blood vessels	dilation *and* constriction	—
Sweat glands	sweating	—
Skin	hairs stand up	—
Pupil of the eye	dilation	constriction
Nose, tear ducts and salivary glands	—	secretion
Bladder	—	stimulates emptying
Alimentary canal	inhibits downward passage of food	promotes downward passage of food, digestion
Male genitals	ejaculation	erection

Neuropsychology – the Study of Brain and Behaviour

The study of how human actions and mental events can be related to processes in the nervous system is known as **neuropsychology**. Current neuropsychology is founded on three main approaches: clinical, experimental human and physiological studies.

Clinical neuropsychology

Clinical neuropsychology is the study of patients with lesions (damage) in the central nervous system. As far as scientific knowledge is concerned, the aim is to understand the normal system by observing what changes occur when faults are introduced. It is not acceptable, certainly in humans, to experimentally remove parts of the nervous system to observe the subsequent effects, and so we must rely upon accidentally occurring changes and gain what information we can from those.

For a little over a century, since it was realized that different behavioural functions were generated by different parts of the cerebral cortex, clinical case material has been systematically collected. This case material comes from patients who have developed tumours of the brain, have contracted cerebral diseases, suffered strokes, or received head injuries. From the scientist's point of view, the more clear-cut and limited (discrete) the lesion, the more useful are the data from that patient. For this reason, patients with cerebral tumours which have been removed at surgery (so that the location and extent of abnormal tissue is precisely known), and patients who have suffered penetrating brain injuries, especially from missile wounds, have been the most actively studied. Clinical neuropsychology has made significant advances following each major war around the world.

In recent years a more rigorous experimental approach has been adopted, so that clinical neuropsychologists now tend to collect a series of similar cases and subject them to a set of carefully controlled laboratory investigations. This means that the findings can be independent of individual variability, and that more precise assessments can be made of which psychological abilities are affected and to what degree. Single-case studies still, however, play a part, and examples of both kinds of study, and the information which they can yield, follow in chapter 3.

The logic of correlating lesion size and location with some breakdown of behaviour (dysfunction), and so inferring the organization of functions in the normal system, is simple. It is however, not so easy to carry out in practice. Apart from the practical difficulties of working with impaired patients, and the rather haphazard way in which clinical case material occurs, certain logical difficulties arise. You may know the (I am sure untrue) story of a scientist who taught a mouse to jump over a hurdle on hearing the command 'jump'. He cut off its legs and found that it no longer jumped at the command, and so he concluded that the mouse was deaf and must hear through its legs. That probably strikes you as silly, but only because you already know quite a lot about mice. If you removed a single component from a television set, and found that there was no longer a picture, would it mean that the component was responsible for generating the picture?

The solution is to find sites which, when damaged, lead to the loss of a particular function, but not others – and also to check that this particular function is not affected by damage to other sites (**double dissociation**). Only then can we be sure that that site is associated with the function. Given the complexity of the brain, this is a difficult undertaking, but one in which progress is being made (Beaumont, 1983; Golden and Vicente, 1983).

Of course clinical neuropsychology is not only concerned with scientific knowledge. It has a real and important practical application in assisting in the diagnosis, treatment and rehabilitation of patients with brain injuries. In fact the major impetus in studying the localization of cerebral functions was the need to use information about behavioural disturbances to help identify the type and location of injury which had occurred. This has become less important with modern brain-imaging techniques, and attention has turned towards rehabilitation.

An accurate psychological description of the patient's functions, both intact and disabled, is essential as the basis of treatment and rehabilitation. This can only follow from a sound understanding of how psychological functions are organized in the brain. It is to provide such descriptions that clinical neuropsychological research is increasingly devoted (Miller, 1984).

Experimental human neuropsychology

Over the last 25 years, techniques have been developed to allow the psychological organization of the human brain in normal subjects to be studied in the laboratory. Studies using these techniques are the basis of **experimental neuropsychology**.

The principal techniques are the divided visual field and dichotic listening methods, which will be described in more detail in chapter 3. They rely, however, on presenting the stimulus material which is relevant to the subject's task so that it is projected into a known area of the brain. The subject's subsequent performance on the task can then be studied as a function of where the information was initially directed. It is then possible to make deductions about how the brain is organized to carry out the task.

These studies can be carried out with stimuli in the visual, auditory and tactile modalities, and common tasks involve simple recognition, matching, or categorization of the stimulus material. The emphasis has therefore been on cognitive processes such as perception, identification, semantic association (the extraction of meaning) and memory. Reading has been a particular topic of research, with interest being shown in whether those suffering from severe reading difficulties (dyslexia) have a brain which is differently organized from that of the successful reader. However, some experiments have also been carried out on emotional responses, when the stimuli presented have often been faces (Beaumont, 1982; Springer and Deutsch, 1985).

Differences in the brain organization of right and left handers have also been studied by these methods. It would seem that such differences are inherited and that the brain of the left hander is less clearly lateralized (has functions less clearly assigned to the left and right sides of the brain) than that of the right hander (Annett, 1985). Similar differences may exist between the sexes, but thse are not so widely accepted.

These studies are mainly cognitive and concern the higher levels of the CNS. Affective (emotional) processes can be studied in the ANS, in an area of research known as **psychophysiology**. Processes in the ANS produce changes in the various peripheral organs which are part of this system. Fortunately these changes are relatively easy to observe and record. Typical measures are of heart rate, sweating, respiration rate, muscle tension, blood pressure and skin temperature (or blushing). Recordings of these measures can be used to study how emotional responses to both physiological and psychological events are governed by the ANS. It has been claimed by some that such recordings can also reveal deception on the part of subjects, but there is considerable scientific opposition to this belief.

Physiological studies

The study of psychological responses in the ANS is psychophysiology; the study of how other fundamental physiological processes influence behaviour is *physiological psychology*. Almost any physiological process, not just those in the nervous system, has some effect upon behaviour. However, psychologists have concentrated on the physiology of the nervous system, and have tended to use one of four approaches in their research (Gale and Edwards, 1983).

The first is the **comparative** approach. The nervous system of animals is examined and *compared* to the human system. Animals are studied because certain experiments can be performed on animals which are regarded as unethical on humans. This may not necessarily involve interference with the animal beyond keeping it in captivity so that its behaviour can be observed. However, animals are also used because most have a much shorter life cycle than humans; because their nervous systems and behaviour may be simpler, and so easier to understand, than the human system; or because they can be observed living in 'natural' conditions in the wild. The human nervous system may also be compared to that of animals in the context of evolutionary development (phylogeny). Seing how the system has evolved may give clues to its structure and functions.

The second approach is the study of **basic neural systems**. The operation of single nerve cells, and groups of interconnected nerve cells, is analysed. This is sometimes referred to as experiment at the **single-cell level**. Some of the research is anatomical, and involves microscopic examination of the structure of different cells and their interconnection. It may extend to mapping the main bundles of fibres passing to and fro in the brain. In the case of certain very simple animals, it may even be possible to map the entire nervous system of the animal. Other research is electrophysiological, in which the electrical activity of groups of cells is directly recorded. Most of this research is performed upon animals and usually involves some experimental interference with the animal. Computer simulation of neural networks is an alternative way of testing out ideas about how neural systems operate.

Electrophysiology is a third approach when used with humans. Here, with the exception of certain surgical patients when electrodes can be inserted into the brain, the recordings of the electrical activity are taken from electrodes placed on the surface of the scalp. Either the on-going activity can be continuously recorded in an **electroencephalogram** (EEG), or else the response of the brain to specific stimuli can be elicited in the form of **average evoked potentials** (these techniques will be discussed further in chapter 4).

The fourth approach is by analysing the **neurochemistry** of the brain. Again, much of the research demands the use of animals. The brain can be regarded as a chemical as much as an electrical machine, and neuroscientists study the various chemicals involved in running the machine, and how they are distributed. A particular field, **neuropharmacology**, is concerned with how drugs change behaviour: in humans as well as animals. Some of these drugs may be used to treat abnormal behaviour; others may change behaviour within the normal range, affecting alertness, anxiety, sociability, appetite, sexual drive, or assertiveness (Silverstone and Turner, 1982).

Neurons and Neural Transmission

The nervous system is made up of a complex network of nerve cells or **neurons**. Not only is the network of these cells and their interconnections complex, but there is also considerable variation in the form which they take. Some basic knowledge of the structure and function of neurons is necessary to understand how the nervous system as a whole operates, and how its processes can be studied.

The structure of the neuron

Although there is great variety in the form of neurons in the nervous system, they all conform to the same general structure. As with all cells, there is a **cell body** which contains the **nucleus**. From the cell body, a number of arms extend. One of these is the **axon** and the others are **dendrites**. A neuron may have few or many dendrites, but has only one axon. In figure 1.7, in which a typical neuron is shown, the axon is very much more prominent than the dendrites, but this is not always the case.

For much of its length, the axon is surrounded by a sheath of **myelin**. The

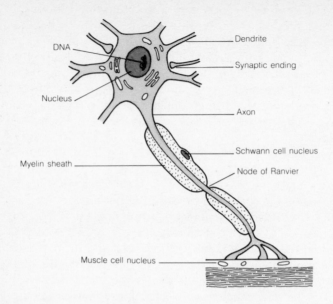

DNA

Dendrite

Synaptic ending

Nucleus

Axon

Schwann cell nucleus

Myelin sheath

Node of Ranvier

Muscle cell nucleus

FIGURE 1.7   *The basic structure of a neuron*

myelin sheath is broken at various points by the **nodes of Ranvier**, so that in cross-section it looks rather like a string of sausages. The myelin can be thought of as insulation around the wiring. It protects the axon, and prevents interference between axons as they pass along in bundles, sometimes thousands at a time.

You will have met the term 'grey matter' for the brain, and there is also 'white matter'. In a section through the brain it is easy to see both grey and white areas. The cortex and other nerve centres are grey, the regions in between, white. The grey coloration is produced by the aggregation of thousands of cell bodies, while the white is the colour of the myelin. The white colour reveals the presence of bundles of axons passing through the brain, rather than areas in which connections are being made.

No neuron has direct connection with any other. At the far end of the axon are a number of **terminal filaments**, and these run up close to other neurons. They may be close to the dendrites of the other neuron (sometimes to special structures called **dendritic spines**), or close to the cell body itself. Where the first neuron comes close to the second neuron, a **synapse** is formed, a space across which the first neuron may communicate with the second.

Although this is the common structure of all nerve cells, there is considerable variety in their appearance. Two of these variations are shown in figure 1.8. There is a similar diversity in the patterns of interconnection among cells. These can be revealed by **staining** sections of the tissue with

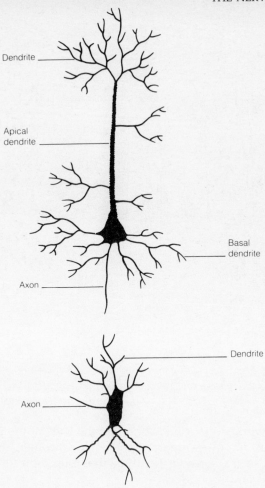

Dendrite

Apical
dendrite

Basal
dendrite

Axon

Dendrite

Axon

FIGURE 1.8   *Two neurons from the cortex of a rabbit, illustrating the variety of form among neurons*

particular substances which under the microscope reveal the presence of, say, cell bodies or myelin. Some examples are shown in figure 1.9. Research is continually revealing that some neurons interconnect in unusual and unexpected ways, adding to the diversity of the system – and the problems of analysing how it works.

Neural transmission

The nervous system is generally thought of as involved in **information processing**, although this is only one way of thinking about (one 'model' of) how it operates. Human-designed information-processing systems are typically electrical or electronic, and so we tend to analyse the operation of

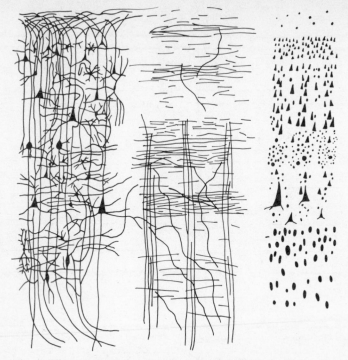

FIGURE 1.9 *Three different types of stain which show: left, the outline of neurons (Golgi stain); centre, myelinated fibres (Weigert stain); right, cell bodies (Nissl stain). These also show different layers in the cortex from the surface (at the top) downwards*

the brain as if it worked in a similar way. At the level of the neuron, we can observe electrical impulses being transmitted through the network of neurons, and it seems sensible to think that this represents information being transmitted and processed.

In its resting state, the membrane surrounding the neuron carries a standing electrical charge. The membrane is relatively positive on the outer surface, and negative on the inner surface in its stable inactive state. It is said to be **polarized**. If this state of equilibrium is disturbed, then the membrane changes state and the inner surface becomes positive with respect to the outside. It becomes **depolarized**. If sufficient depolarization occurs, then this change in activity will develop into an **action potential** which will be propagated along the length of the axon. This **propagation** occurs because the depolarization disturbs the next part of the membrane, allowing the action potential to develop there, which in turn disturbs the next part of the membrane, and so on.

Meanwhile, the section of axon first depolarized **repolarizes**, so that the outer surface again becomes positive with respect to the inner surface. The first stage of repolarization actually involves a short period when the outer surface is unusually positive – a period of **hyperpolarization** – after which it returns to the normal resting state. During hyperpolarization, the neuron is in a **refractory** state, and a further action potential cannot be generated until the normal resting state has been re-established.

The normal resting potential is typically between 40 and 100 millivolts. The progression of changes at a given point in the axon can be represented by the graph shown in figure 1.10 (beware: physiologists often adopt the convention of negative-up and positive-down in graphs; here the normal physical convention of positive-up is observed). The graph shows the successive changes in the potential difference across the membrane of the neuron.

Another way to think of the changes is in terms of the state of the various parts of an axon in which an action potential has been propagated. In figure 1.11 a schematic action potential is passing from left to right along the section of an axon. The relative state of the inner and outer surfaces as positive or negative is shown. The action potential has not yet reached the extreme right, so the axon is still in its resting state. The action potential has just reached the preceding section which is therefore active. The section before that, which the action potential has just passed, is in the hyperpolarized refractory state, while the part at the extreme left has had chance to return to the resting state after the passage of the potential.

Conduction speeds vary enormously in different types of neuron, but in the PNS, for example, action potentials travel along motor fibres at between 60 and 100 metres per second. In nerves serving pain, temperature and position senses, transmission is rather slower at between 12 and 30 metres

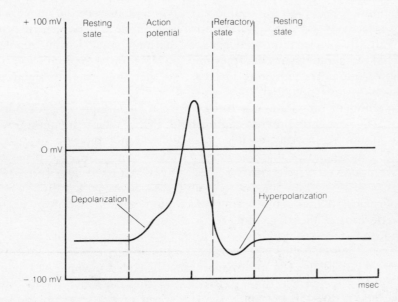

FIGURE 1.10   *An action potential seen as the changes over time in electrical potential at a given point on the axon*

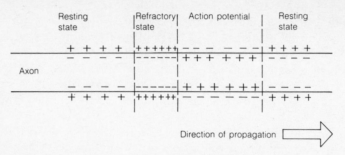

FIGURE 1.11   *A diagram of the cross-section through an axon as an action potential passes from left to right, showing the pattern of positive and negative ionization*

per second. In myelinated fibres the potential may not pass at a steady rate but jump from node to node along the axon by **saltatory** conduction. This presumably allows the potential to pass more rapidly than would otherwise be possible.

These electrical changes in the membrane surrounding the neuron are accomplished by chemical processes (so that it is sensible to think of the brain as a chemical, as well as an electrical, machine). In the resting state there are negative protein anions and some positive potassium ions inside the membrane, and positive sodium ions with some negative chlorine ions outside the membrane. Some of the potassium and chlorine ions can cross the membrane to maintain the equilibrium. When disturbed, the membrane becomes selectively permeable to the positive sodium ions (which rush in) so changing the potential difference across the membrane. During repolarization, the membrane again becomes impermeable to the sodium ions, but now allows the potassium ions to cross, so that they rush out and re-establish the resting potential.

This method of operation has three important consequences for nerve impulses. The first is that there is a **threshold**, below which the neuron will not fire. If not sufficiently excited, the cell will not develop an action potential. The second is that the effect is **all-or-none**. The size of action potentials in a given type of neuron does not vary. There is either an action potential or no action potential: no gradations in size occur. Thirdly, there is a **refractory period** after firing during which the neuron may not fire again. The rate of firing is therefore limited.

These factors mean that information must be transmitted by the temporal pattern of the pulses (or 'spikes' as they tend to appear on an oscilloscope) of the action potentials. The information must be coded in some way into a train of pulses which are then passed along the axon and on to other neurons and so through the network. The speed of transmission through the network will be limited by the various refractory periods of the individual neurons in the network.

When the action potential reaches the end of the axon it arrives at a synapse where it causes a chemical to be released. This chemical, a **neurotransmitter** substance, crosses the gap between the two neurons, and affects the neuron at the other side of the synapse. This effect can be either **excitatory** or **inhibitory**. If it is excitatory, then it will increase the chances of an action potential developing in the second neuron. If it is inhibitory, it will decrease the chances of an action potential in the second neuron.

In simple terms it is easiest to think of the action potential in a single axon (the **presynaptic** neuron) arriving at a synapse, and having an excitatory effect which triggers off an action potential in another (**postsynaptic**) neuron, and so passing some message on. No doubt this does occur, but the typical situation is of any neuron having synaptic connections with many others, perhaps hundreds. The activity in any neuron is therefore the **summation** of the influences of many other neurons which synapse with it. Some of these influences will be excitatory and others will be inhibitory. This is why you should think of an action potential arriving at a synpase as increasing (if excitatory) or decreasing (if inhibitory) the *probability* of activity in the neuron beyond the synapse, rather than it having a definite effect.

Consider the myriad interconnections in the central nervous system, where there are at least 10 thousand million neurons in the brain alone. Each cell has synaptic connections with several, and often many, others. These connections may be either excitatory or inhibitory. To add to the complexity remember that if two neurons (*A* and *B*) synapse with a third neuron (*C*), there may well be an interaction between *A* and *B*. *A* may enhance or inhibit the effect of *B* upon *C* by the synapses which *A* has with *B*. You will start to see just how complex is the structure of the CNS when considered at the level of single nerve cells. You will realize what an immense task it is to analyze the operation of the system, and yet what an exciting challenge it is to discover how this system generates ideas, images, inventions, dreams, emotions and all the rest of human experience.

Neurotransmitters

Neurotransmitters form the essential link in passing neural activity from neuron to neuron. The neurotransmitter substance is generated by structures within the presynaptic neuron (figure 1.12). The arrival of an action potential triggers the release of the transmitter chemical into the gap between the neurons – the **synaptic cleft**. The transmitter then binds on to chemical sites in the postsynaptic membrane, causing changes which may result in a postsynaptic potential. There are also biochemical systems which mop up unused transmitter substance around the synapse and pass useful constituents back into the presynaptic neuron. Others regulate both the production of the substance and its effect at the postsynaptic receptor site.

Transmitter substances can be studied in several ways. One is by observing the effects of drugs which can modify the operation of the neurotransmitter at the synapse. Some drugs can mimic the effects of the

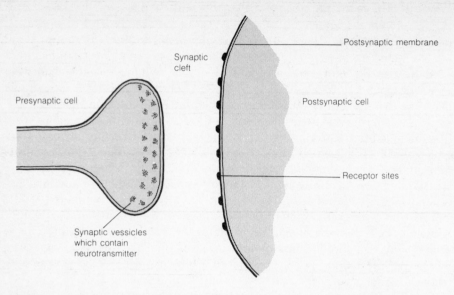

FIGURE 1.12   *A schematic view of a synapse*

neurotransmitter at the postsynaptic membrane so making the relevant synapses more active. Others can promote or inhibit the production or release of transmitter substance. The availability of the transmitter in the synaptic cleft can also be modified. These methods are used to develop a knowledge of the substances which act as transmitters, and the chemicals which are involved in their synthesis and regulation. In turn, observed changes in behaviour can be related to the administration of these substances. In this way, different neurotransmitters can be associated with different behavioural functions.

Another way of studying neurotransmitters is by labelling techniques. Substances can be administered which are easy to observe and which will chemically bind on to the neurotransmitter which is under investigation. Observation may be by microscopic detection of the radioactivity or fluorescence of the substance, which thus acts as a marking label of the presence of the neurotransmitter. In this way, synapses which operate by using particular neurotransmitters can be mapped out.

A number of different transmitter substances have been identified, and they include: acetylcholine, adrenalin and noradrenaline (known as 'epine-phrine' and 'norepinephrine' in America), dopamine, gamma-aminobutyric acid (GABA) and serotonin (Van Toller, 1983).

Acetylcholine is used in systems which control muscular activity and is found widely in the PNS, although it is also used in certain pathways within the brain. Adrenaline, noradenaline and dopamine are members of a group known as the catecholamines, of which noradrenaline is perhaps the most important. Among other functions, these neurotransmitters are involved in the control of mood. Amphetamine is thought to block the mechanism by which noradrenaline can be taken up to be reused, and other chemicals which affect noradrenergic synapses (using noradrenaline) are used in the control of psychiatric mood disorders.

Drugs which block the action of dopamine have been used in the treatment of schizophrenia, suggesting that this transmitter is involved in systems controlling normal patterns of thinking. Patients with Parkinson's disease (see p. 6) can be successfully treated by drugs which increase the amount of dopamine available at synapses which use this transmitter, suggesting that these dopaminergic synapses operate inefficiently in patients with the disease (Pincus and Tucker, 1978).

Serotonin is involved in various behavioural systems, one of which is the pattern of sleep and wakefulness. Drugs which produce hallucinations are also thought to act at sites where serotonin is normally active.

What is important about neurotransmitters is that they are organized into systems which are related to particular behavioural functions. These systems can be identified in the brain and linked to anatomical neural structures and the pathways among them. Knowing about these systems, and the chemicals which are involved in them, allows drugs to be developed which will modify the systems and allow behavioural abnormalities to be corrected.

Hormones

Basic structure of the endocrine system

The endocrine system of hormones in the body is not strictly part of the nervous system. However, it has such intimate links with the nervous system that the two can be considered together.

The endocrine system is composed of internal glands which secrete particular substances – hormones – into the blood stream. The blood stream carries them to almost every cell of the body. This allows the hormones to have a widespread influence and so control the overall function of the body by regulating basic metabolic processes. The endocrine system and the ANS work together in the generalized control of behaviour.

The principle behind the control which the hormones exercise is **homeostasis**. A simple feedback loop maintains the bodily processes at a predetermined level. If the process becomes overactive, this is detected and the release of hormone is reduced so that the process also becomes less active. If the activity in the process falls below the predetermined level, this is also detected, and results in an increase in the amount of hormone released, which in turn increases the activity back up to the correct level.

There are eight major endocrine glands, or pairs of glands. They are shown in figure 1.13, and their main functions are listed in table 1.2. Although all the endocrine glands have some influence on behaviour, those of particular interest to psychologists are the pituitary gland (sometimes called the 'hypophysis'), the adrenal glands and the gonads.

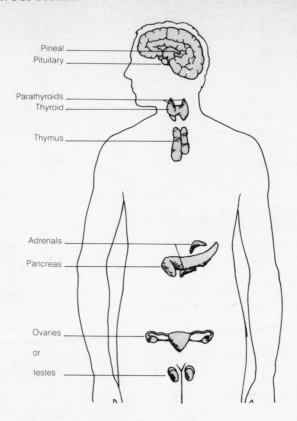

FIGURE 1.13   *The location of the principal endocrine glands (From Taylor et al., 1982)*

Links between the nervous and endocrine systems

Both the pituitary gland and the adrenal glands have important direct links with the nervous system. In particular, the pituitary gland has very rich connections with the hypothalamus. This is particularly significant because the pituitary gland plays a role in co-ordinating the function of other glands in the endocrine system.

Some of the hormones which the pituitary produces have an indirect effect by regulating the production and release of other hormones. For this reason, it is often regarded as the 'master gland' of the system. Several of the endocrine glands secrete more than one type of hormone: the pituitary, for instance, secretes at least six different hormones. Certain of these influence the activity of the adrenals and the gonads as well as the thyroid. The hormones which these glands then release into the blood stream are subsequently detected as they circulate, not only in the pituitary, but also in the blood supply to the hypothalamus itself.

As the pituitary has direct links with the hypothalamus, it also has strong

TABLE 1.2 *Major functions of the principal endocrine glands (their location is shown in figure 1.13)*

Gland	Function
Pineal	poorly understood; may be concerned with first onset of menstruation in girls
Pituitary	acts as 'master gland', but also controls growth and water balance and secretion
Parathyroid	supervises calcium metabolism and general levels of activation in the nervous system
Thyroid	controls metabolic rate and therefore activity and fatigue and body weight; has influence on emotion
Thymus	affects the lymphoid system and immune reactions, providing physiological protection for the body
Adrenals	produce life-maintaining regulators (steroids); supervise salt and carbohydrate metabolism; affect emotion by release of adrenaline and noradrenaline
Pancreas	controls sugar metabolism by insulin
Gonads	(male testes, female ovaries) maintain reproductive state and govern sexual appearance

structural and functional connections with the whole of the autonomic nervous system. One illustration of these links is in the mechanisms which are involved in hypertension. Hypertension is abnormally raised blood pressure in persons susceptible to psychological stress. Some of the components of this system are shown in figure 1.14.

Psychological processes in the brain such as anxiety, emotional tension and other mental stresses have an influence on subcortical structures including the thalamus and hypothalamus. Discharges from the hypothalamus act upon brain stem mechanisms which raise heart rate and elevate blood pressure. They also pass into the ANS with two main results: arteries become constricted, and the inner part of the adrenal gland (adrenal medulla) releases noradrenaline, both further increasing blood pressure. The hypothalamus also acts upon the pituitary gland which releases a substance which stimulates the outer part of the adrenal gland (adrenal cortex). This in turn produces metabolic changes which further increase blood pressure, partly by factors acting upon the kidney. Even in this very simplified example, you may begin to see how rich and complex are these interactions between the endocrine and nervous systems.

The adrenal glands play an important role in the psychological responses of stress and fear, partly because of the direct control of the adrenal medulla by the sympathetic branch of the ANS. The adrenal medulla produces both adrenaline and noradrenaline (hence the names). These substances (already noted as neurotransmitters) can have effects which include:

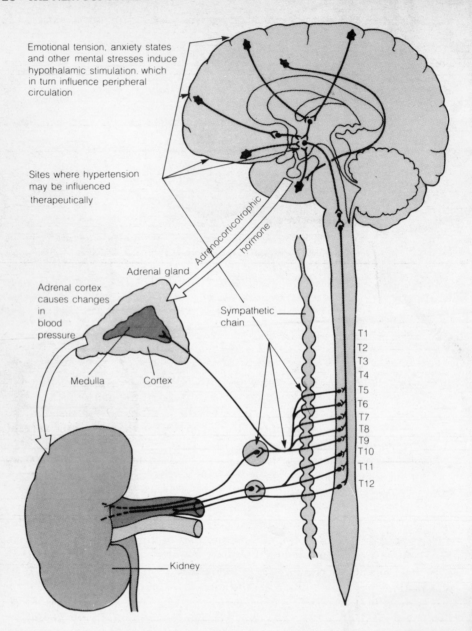

Emotional tension, anxiety states and other mental stresses induce hypothalamic stimulation, which in turn influence peripheral circulation

Sites where hypertension may be influenced therapeutically

Adrenocorticotrophic hormone

Adrenal gland

Adrenal cortex causes changes in blood pressure

Sympathetic chain

Medulla   Cortex

T1
T2
T3
T4
T5
T6
T7
T8
T9
T10
T11
T12

Kidney

FIGURE 1.14 *Some of the elements of the nervous and endocrine systems involved in hypertension (Amended from an illustration by F. Netter MD(c). Reproduced by courtesy of Ciba-Geigy PLC Basle. All rights reserved)*

an increase in heart rate and blood volume;

contraction of the spleen, so releasing more red blood cells;

release of stored sugar from the liver, for energy;

redistribution of the blood supply, in readiness for muscular activity;

deepening of respiration;

dilation of the pupils;

an increase in the blood's ability to coagulate;

and an increase in lymphocytes, to aid in bodily repair after damage.

These add up to a massive and general mobilization of bodily resources which can be achieved in a matter of seconds. It is just what we should expect to be associated with activity in the sympathetic branch of the ANS.

These are short-term changes in bodily response to arousal. They are what you may well have experienced immediately after a 'close shave' which nearly resulted in a road traffic accident. It generally comes immediately *after*, because of the time it takes the system to respond. Our bodies did not evolve to respond to events happening when we travel at 60 m.p.h.! In the 'natural' environment, the ANS and the endocrine system would together prepare the body for flight, or active defence and any necessary subsequent repair, as rapidly as is necessary (Cox et al., 1983).

Unfortunately, prolonged and severe stress may lead to other long-term changes in this system. If the pituitary becomes overactive in its production of the hormone which affects the adrenal cortex, then there will be a general increase in the levels of hormone which the adrenal cortex then releases (cortisone, hydrocortisone, or corticosterone). These result in the transfer of non-sugars into sugars and sensitize blood vessels to the effects of adrenaline and noradrenaline; effects which contribute to the general sympathetic response to stress. However, these hormones also have some undesired effects: they may reduce the ability of the body to combat damage; they may reduce the resistance to infection; and they may both halt bodily growth and interfere with sexual and reproductive activity. This is one way in which serious stress, even of a purely psychological kind, may result in a shut-down of certain bodily activities, and may be the cause of **psychosomatic illnesses** (Warwick Evans, 1983). (An experiment reporting that physiological response of young children under stress is presented in box 1.1.)

The sex hormones

The gonads produce the sex hormones. The male gonads are the testes and produce **androgens** of which the most important is **testosterone**. The female gonads, the ovaries, produce **oestrogens** and **progesterone**. Although males have a predominance of androgens, and females a predominance of oestro-gens, *both* types of hormone are present in both sexes. The adrenal glands are partly responsible for supplying the hormone typical of the opposite sex.

The sex hormones, as you might expect, control the maintenance of the reproductive organs, and in the female oestrogens maintain the monthly oestrus cycle. Progesterone is the gestational hormone preparing the uterus for pregnancy and organizing milk production. There are, however, less obvious effects. Testosterone promotes the synthesis of proteins, and aids tissue growth and repair. Oestrogens promote the breakdown of proteins into other substances, and lead to fatty tissue being deposited (resulting in the softer average body shape of females). They may produce weight gain and also reduce the level of cholesterol in the blood (which is why women are less prone to heart attacks).

These opposing effects of androgens and oestrogens emphasize the importance of remembering that there is no dichotomy between 'male' androgens and 'female' oestrogens. There is a balance in the body between the two types of sex hormone, a balance which differs between the sexes. This difference is of course an average difference: it is is clear to see that males vary between being extremely 'masculine' and rather 'feminine' in appearance, and that there is is corresponding variation in females. This is partly related to the levels of the sex hormones circulating in the blood, particularly during the early stages of development (Vowles, 1980).

Research has shown that sexual differentiation – developing as a male or a female – depends upon a critical period early in prenatal development. The sex hormones have an important influence throughout early development on later physiological appearance and function. We also know that the level of sex hormones increases again at puberty, and brings about mature sexual appearance and reproductive capability. Experiments in which animals have their gonads removed at various stages of development (so removing the source of androgens or oestrogens), and have implantations or injections to replace the lost hormones by either the sex-appropriate or sex-inappropriate hormones, enable the effects of these hormones on development to be studied (see box 1.2). Certain abnormalities and diseases enable similar effects to be observed in human patients.

Not only physical appearance and sexual function are related to the sex hormones both present during development and currently circulating in the body; general aspects of behaviour are also to some degree related to androgens and oestrogens. Sexual drive and potency can be enhanced by androgens and decreased by oestrogens, but other less directly reproductive activities may also be affected. Aggression can be related to the levels of testosterone present in the body and the effects may extend to psychological hostility. Although it is less certain, some researchers have argued that androgens may also be responsible for ambition and drive. There is certainly good reason to believe that the sex hormones have some part to play, amongst a host of other influences, in the formation of human personality (Singleton, 1978).

The endocrine system therefore operates alongside the nervous system. There are direct links, and a host of interacting mutual influences between the two. The endocrine system, in particular, works in co-operation with the autonomic nervous system to provide generalized control over the level of bodily activity, and to maintain appropriate levels of physical and mental arousal. (Further aspects of arousal will be discussed in chapter 4.)

Further reading

A sound and clear introductory text on physiological psychology is J. W. Kalat (1984), *Biological Psychology* (2nd edn), Belmont, Calif.: Wadsworth. It contains useful coverage of the general structure of the nervous system, of neurons and neuronal transmission, and of the role of hormones in development and in sexual behaviour. A readable guide to the structure and functions of the nervous system and nervous tissue is provided by R. F. Thompson (1985), *The Brain: An Introduction to Neuroscience*, San Francisco: W. H. Freeman. A reasonably non-technical introduction to the functions of the ANS and how they can be measured in humans, including some discussion of typical findings, is J. Hassett (1978), *A Primer of Psychophysiology*, San Francisco: W. H. Freeman. Probably the best text to cover all aspects of nervous system structure and function at an introductory level is B. Kolb and I. Q. Whishaw (1985), *Fundamentals of Human Neuropsychology* (2nd edn), San Francisco: W. H. Freeman.

Discussion points

1 Discuss, in a group, the physical experiences which follow a sudden shock or fright. How do these experiences relate to what you know of the operation of the ANS?

2 What can be learned from the study of brain-damaged patients, and what are the limitations of this approach?

3 How important is the study of animals in understanding the human nervous system?

4 How do you suppose the pattern of simple inhibitory and excitatory influences of single neurons can be built up to produce complex thought? (speculate freely)

5 Men and women differ in their behaviour. Is it possible to tell how much this is due to biological, rather than social, factors?

Practical exercises

1 On an unlabelled diagram of the nervous system, or on a model if one is available, identify each of the main structures in the CNS mentioned in this chapter.

2 Perform a simple experiment to assess the effect of emotional arousal on heart rate as an indicator of ANS function. Heart rate is easily recorded by counting the pulse at the wrist. The pulse is usually prominent just under, or a little above and forward of, where the buckle on a wrist-watch falls. It will be better to enlist the help of a subject other than yourself (but make sure, in advance, that they are willing and prepared to be mildly upset during the experiment). Assess the normal heart rate under 'resting' conditions, and then observe the effects of thinking about particularly frightening or upsetting events (your subject doesn't need to tell you what they find distressing, but must be willing to concentrate on whatever that is, when instructed). If you have to suggest something, try: thinking about surgical operations, motor accidents, spiders, or physical attack. Contrast the periods of arousal with periods of relaxation (thinking about lying on a sunny beach or by a babbling brook; dozing in an armchair after a pleasant meal; lying in the bath after a long and energetic walk).

You might also try using pictures as evoking stimuli, if you can find suitably upsetting or relaxing material. You might also ask subjects after each period how upset or relaxed they felt.

Design the experiment so that periods of rest come between the periods of arousal or relaxation, and that these occur in a random or balanced order. You may wish to repeat the experiment with a number of subjects.

Does heart rate differ under the different conditions of arousal? Which produces more change: imagining events, or seeing pictures? Does the heart rate change relate to how much emotional change the subject reported? How large is the change in comparison with, say, running on the spot for a minute?

(See P. J. Lang, M. J. Kozak, G. A. Miller and A. McLean, Jr (1980), Emotional imagery: concept-structure and patterns of somato-visceral response, *Psychophysiology*, 17, 179–92.)

3 Another easily assessed index of emotional change as expressed in ANS function is the diameter of the pupil of the eye. Observers are known to unconsciously use information about changes in pupil diameter (pupillary dilation – when enlarged – or constriction – when smaller) when judging emotional state.

Obtain some suitable photographs or magazine cuttings clearly showing the face. Produce a number of versions with pupils enlarged or reduced ('Tipp-Ex', ink and a photocopier would all be useful). There is no need to make the changes too dramatic! Ask subjects to judge the resulting images in terms of how excited, happy, upset, anxious and afraid they appear. Subjects could use a rating scale from 1 to 7. You might give the different versions of the same face to the same, or to different, subjects.

Are more extreme emotions attributed to the faces with pupils enlarged or reduced? Which direction of change is associated with each emotion? Were subjects aware that the pupils had been tampered with – and if so, does it matter?

You might also note, while you have the stimuli, that subjects with enlarged pupils are often judged more physically attractive. Is this also true for the images you have prepared?

(See M. P. Janisse (1977) *Pupillometry*, Washington, DC: Hemisphere Publishing Corporation.)

Box 1.1

Sex differences in behaviour pattern and catecholamine and cortisol excretion in three- to six-year-old day-care children

The aim of this study was to look for possible neuroendocrine changes related to what might be a stressful experience for children – attendance at a new day-care centre. As part of a wider study into sex differences in neuroendocrine activity in children, Lundberg examined the excretion of adrenaline and noradrenaline by children aged three to six years.

Eleven children, eight boys and three girls, were the subjects newly attending the centre, although five had had previous experience of day-care. All made normal behavioural adjustment to the day-care situation within the first two weeks.

The measurements of adrenaline and noradrenaline excretion were made from urine, and all urine passed between 8 a.m. and 4 p.m. was collected for analysis: on weekdays at the centre, and during weekends at home. The procedures for urine collection were designed to be non-stressful, and as similar as possible at the centre and at home.

The adrenaline and noradrenaline excreted was measured in terms of *pmol/min*. However, because physically larger children produce more of these substances, the measurements had to be adjusted for the child's size. The estimated body surface area (in m^2) was taken to be an index of size, and so the final measurements are in terms of pmol/min per m^2 or *pmol/min/m^2*. Mean values were calculated for boys and girls, at the centre and at home, for each of the first three weeks at the centre.

The design therefore has three independent variables: sex (boys vs. girls); location (centre vs. home); and week of attendance (1, 2 or 3). The dependent variables are the average quantities of adrenaline and noradrenaline excreted, adjusted for body surface area.

The mean values of adrenaline and noradrenaline excreted by boys and girls over the three weeks are shown in box table 1.1.1. Among the boys, secretion was relatively high during weeks 1 and 3. However, the use of *t*-tests showed that the only significant difference was the decline between weeks 1 and 2 for noradrenaline ($t = 2.94$, df = 7, $p < 0.05$). No consistent pattern was found for the girls.

The means for the days at the centre and at home are shown in box figure 1.1.1. In the at-home condition, boys excreted more adrenaline ($t = 2.96$, $p < 0.01$) and noradrenaline ($t = 3.56$, $p < 0.01$) than the girls. At the day centre, they did so for noradrenaline ($t = 2.28$, $p < 0.05$) but not adrenaline ($t = 1.32$, $p > 0.05$). Adrenaline

Based on material in U. Lundberg, *Biological Psychology*, 16 (1983), 109–17.

BOX TABLE 1.1.1   *Means and standard errors for adrenaline and noradrenaline excretion for boys and girls during the first three weeks at a day-care centre*

	Week number 1			Week number 2			Week number 3		
	Mean	S.E.	N	Mean	S.E.	N	Mean	S.E.	N
Adrenaline excretion (pmol/min/m^2)									
Boys	21.4	3.9	8	18.8	3.8	8	19.5	3.5	8
Girls	15.7	2.6	3	16.8	3.9	3	15.2	1.4	3
Noradrenaline excretion (pmol/min/m^2)									
Boys	80.6	9.0	8	63.8	7.1	8	80.2	14.1	8
Girls	72.6	8.4	3	68.0	7.9	3	57.5	6.3	3

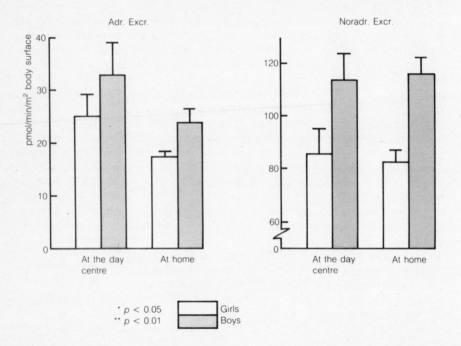

* $p < 0.05$ Girls
** $p < 0.01$ Boys

BOX FIGURE 1.1.1   *Means and standard errors for adrenaline and noradrenaline (eight hours) excretion by boys and girls at a day-care centre and at home*

excretion at the centre was significantly higher than at home in both boys ($t = 2.22$, $p < 0.05$) and girls ($t = 2.28$, $p < 0.05$), but there were no corresponding differences in noradrenaline excretion.

The findings show that the day centre conditions induce elevated levels of adrenaline but not noradrenaline excretion. Adrenaline is thought to be related to emotional, and noradrenaline to physical, stress. The data therefore suggest raised mental rather than physical arousal at the centre: what might be expected when meeting many new people, playing new games and being bombarded by high noise levels. These data do not necessarily indicate distress or anxiety (and there are other data which suggest the children were not unhappy). The raised levels were higher in the first week for the boys, although not for the girls.

The boys excreted more of both substances than the girls during normal self-directed activities and there is reason to think that this is related to sex differences in behaviour patterns. As the children were more free to choose activities at home, this may account for the larger sex differences found in the at-home condition. Boys may actively expose themselves to higher physiological arousal, and this may have an influence on subsequent development.

The two strengths of this study are that a direct measure is taken of the physiological changes which occur, and that a relatively natural stress-inducing context has been studied. It is not always feasible for psychologists to directly measure the changes which occur in neuroendocrine systems in humans, but when it is possible the results are of particular interest. The more natural the situation in which the changes are observed, the more confidence can be had in the validity of the findings.

Against this must be set some weaknesses of the study. The number of subjects is small, and even smaller when divided into boys and girls. It is not clear whether first attending the day-care centre resulted in a really stressful situation for the children or not. It is also not entirely satisfactory to use the weekend days at home as a control for the days at the centre during the week. In some ways it might have been better to study independent groups of children at home and at a day centre, both during weekdays and both undertaking similar activities with similar meals. This would probably, however, have required larger groups to account for the general differences in the individual level of secretion between the groups. As it is, the results are not entirely clear-cut, and the authors recognize that the differences which have been observed may be as much due to differences in activity between home and day centre as in the relative stressfulness of the two situations.

Box 1.2

Exposure of female mouse fetuses of various ages to testosterone and the later activation of intraspecific fighting

It is known that fighting behaviour can be artificially induced in female mice by the administration of testosterone. The aim of this study was to see whether additional prenatal exposure to testosterone might increase the fighting which could be induced in this way. Mice can be exposed to testosterone prenatally by injecting the mother while pregnant, since the hormone passes from the mother into the bloodstream of the baby mice.

In this study, pregnant laboratory-bred mice were injected with either 1 mg of testosterone dissolved in 0.05 ml of sesame oil, or just the oil alone. The oil injection acted as a control for the effects of handling and giving the injection. Half of the mice receiving testosterone, and all the mice receiving oil, had a single injection on day 10 (since conception), day 12, day 14, day 16, or day 18. The other half of the mice receiving testosterone had two injections on days 9 and 10, days 11 and 12, days 13 and 14, days 15 and 16, or days 17 and 18. The pups were born at around 19 days after conception. They were removed from the mother on the day of birth, and between four and six of the females in the litter placed with an untreated foster mother. This ensured that any effects of the injection were due to changes in the pups and not in the behaviour of the mother. The young were weaned on day 21 and had their ovaries removed, under anaesthesia, on day 60. This removed the effects of normally circulating oestrogens in these young adult female animals.

On day 74, a length of tubing containing 5 mg of testosterone in 0.02 ml of oil was implanted below the skin. The testosterone is slowly and continuously absorbed and is known to reliably induce fighting in female mice. The tests for fighting behaviour began two days later and were continued for up to 60 days or until fighting was produced. The test involved placing a male, whose sense of smell had been previously removed, in the cage with the female for ten minutes. These males were used because they neither initiate fights, nor retaliate, but act as a stimulus which will trigger fighting in normal males or in the testosterone-treated females. The criterion for fighting having been elicited was 5 sec of biting and chasing the stimulus animal.

In this design the independent variables are treated prenatally vs. oil-control; the timing of prenatal treatment; and for the testosterone-treated group a single vs. double injection. The dependent variables are the number of animals fighting after having

Based on material in R. Gandelman, C. Rosenthal and S. M. Howard, *Physiology and Behaviour*, 25 (1980), 333–5. Copyright 1980, Pergamon Press Ltd.

testosterone implanted (on day 74), and the number of days before the first fight, or the 'latency' of fighting.

The number of females in each group fighting after testosterone implantation is shown in box table 1.2.1. There were no differences among the oil-treated animals according to day of injection, so their results were pooled for analysis. There were also no differences between offspring exposed to a single or double dose at a similar period, so these results were also pooled in the table (e.g. a single injection on day 14 and injections on days 13 and 14: T-14/13&14).

The later the exposure to testosterone prenatally, the higher the proportion fighting in adult life. Analysis of the proportions in the upper part of box table 1.2.1 yielded a significant chi-squared value (chi-squared = 14.02, df = 5, $p < 0.01$). Dividing the animals into two groups: oil-treated control and injection before day 13, and injection on day 13 or later (lower part of box table 1.2.1) also showed a significant value for chi-squared (12.42, df = 1, $p < 0.01$).

The mean latency to fighting following testosterone implantation as adults is shown in box figure 1.2.1. As the latency scores were not normally distributed, they were transformed by taking the square root of the number of days to first fighting. These transformed values appear in the box figure 1.2.1.

Analysis of variance of these data revealed differences among the groups ($F = 2.74$, df = 10, 207, p < 0.01). Further analysis showed that the animals born of

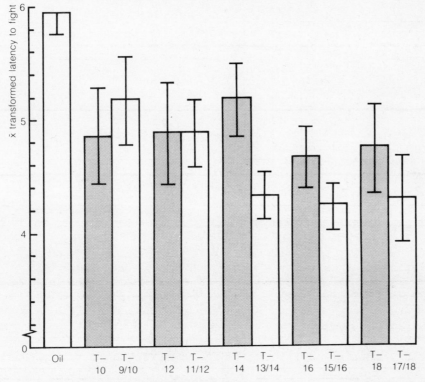

BOX FIGURE 1.2.1 *Mean transformed latencies (days) to fight following the initiation of testosterone (T) treatment during adult life. Female mice were exposed as fetuses to T (via maternal injection) on one or two days of gestation. Other females were exposed only to the oil vehicle. Vertical bars indicate SE*

BOX TABLE 1.2.1   *The proportion (and percentage) of female mice that fought as a consequence of chronic testosterone (T) treatment*

		Group					
	Oil	T-10/9&10	T-12/11&12	T-14/13&14	T-16/15&16	T-18/17&18
Proportion fighting (%)	63/87 (72)	34/48 (70)	28/43 (65)	43/50 (86)	35/39 (89)	35/40 (87)
Total		125/178 (70)			113/129 (87)	

Animals either were exposed to oil or T prior to birth. Each T-exposed group is composed of 2 subgroups: mice born of mother given 1 or 2 injections of T during pregnancy Group T-10/9&10, for example, consists of mice born of mothers administered T either on day 10 or on days 9 and 10 of gestation mothers injected on days 13 and 14, days 15 and 16, day 16, or days 17 and 18 fought significantly sooner than those born of mothers injected earlier.

The results support previous findings that if the normal source of female hormones is removed in adult female mice, and the male hormone testosterone is introduced, then the females will behave like male animals and will show aggression to other males. Further, if the animals are exposed to testosterone before birth, but after the 13th day since conception, the effect of testosterone being introduced in adult life is that a greater proportion of the females will fight. If they receive a double dose after day 13 (or on day 16 alone) the effect will appear significantly more quickly.

This study illustrates the importance of circulating sex hormones in aggressive behaviour in adult life, and also shows that prenatal exposure to sex hormones can have an influence on later development. The latter also illustrates a *critical period* effect, since the prenatal exposure was only effective between day 13 after conception and birth. This is a well-designed study in which all the appropriate experimental controls have been included. There is good reason to have confidence in the reliability of the findings. The difficulty is to assess their relevance to human aggression. Even for mice, the experimental situation in which the tests are carried out and the housing in which the mice are placed are relatively unnatural. Although the results tell us something very interesting about mice, it is not clear whether they can be applied to humans acting within a very much richer social and interpersonal context. It may be that the circulating level of sex hormones does have an influence on human aggression, but it would be unwise to think that studies of this kind do more than hint at the possibility of such an effect.

2

Sensation and Perception

Our feeling of living in a real, solid and stable physical world is extremely powerful. We generally seem to be in contact with the environment which surrounds us. It may take some effort to realize that we are really only in contact with a world which our mind has interpreted and re-created.

Physical stimuli arrive at peripheral receptors and are converted into **sensations**. These sensations are then passed upwards through the nervous system, and are interpreted so that they become meaningful **perceptions**. Sensations derived from all the senses, and perceptions based upon them, are combined within the brain to build up the vivid representation of the environment which is the basis of our conscious awareness.

Happily, for most of the time, this representation is accurate and accords well with events in the physical world. We reach out a hand towards some object and when we see the hand arrive at the object we feel the touch of contact. Our perceptions seem real, but they are in fact only illusions which *represent* the physical world. Psychologists are interested in how the physical stimuli which the body can detect are transformed into sensations and perception, giving us the rich conscious awareness which we possess.

Although there are many senses, the most effective and important in humans are vision and hearing (audition). These are also the most studied by psychologists, and this chapter will concentrate on just these two senses.

The Visual System

Structure of the visual system

The special receptor which receives visual stimuli is, of course, the eye. The eye is really a specialized part of the brain, pushed out along a stalk to the front of the head – and this is one reason why eye injuries can have such serious consequences. It is in essence simply a sphere with a **lens** at the front, a variable aperture (the **pupil**) to control the amount of light entering

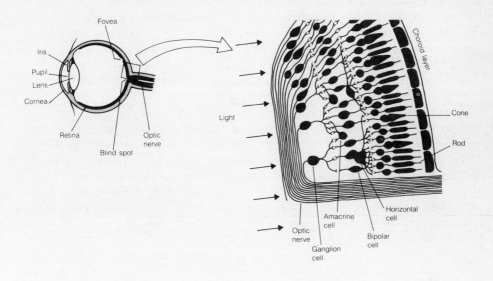

FIGURE 2.1 *A diagrammatic section through the eye and a section through the retina at the edge of the blind spot (From* Introduction to Psychology, *8th edition, by Rita L. Atkinson, Richard C. Atkinson and Ernest R. Hilgard, copyright © 1983 by Harcourt Brace Jovanovich, Inc. Reprinted by permission of the publisher)*

the eye, and a surface capable of detecting light (the **retina**) at the back (see figures 1.5 and 2.1).

The eye is sometimes likened to a camera, but except that it has a lens, an aperture and reacts to light, there is little similarity. The camera passively detects images captured at a fleeting moment in time, even with a cine film or video recording. The eye is much more active in responding to stimulation, and in processing the stimulus in terms of the information which it contains, as we shall see in the next section. It is also in continuous contact with the physical stimuli which fall upon the eye.

The eyeball can be moved in its socket (the orbit), and there are muscles which change the shape of the lens by **accommodation** so that stimuli from objects at different distances can be focused upon the retina. The pupil is also used to limit the light entering the eye, so that the retinal detectors are not swamped by incoming stimulation. Much of the control of the pupil is reflex so that it automatically closes down when the light becomes too bright, and opens up when the general level of light dims. You can see this in operation if you take a subject into a dimly lit room and then suddenly shine a torch at the eye or quickly draw back a curtain.

When the light falls upon the retina at the back of the eye, it is detected by two sorts of receptor: **rods** and **cones** (see figure 2.1). The cones are more numerous near the centre of vision, and are particularly dense in a region known as the **fovea**. The fovea forms a pit in which the cones are very tightly packed and is the region in **central** vision which gives us high **acuity** (very fine resolution). In looking around the world we direct our gaze so that the focus of attention falls over the fovea and provides the best quality of vision. By contrast, rods are more numerous further away from the fovea in **peripheral** areas of the retina.

The light is detected because it causes chemical changes in pigments contained in the receptors. The cones contain one of three photopigments, called **iodopsins**, which are sensitive to different wavelengths of light and so are capable of providing colour vision. The rods contain only one photopigment, **rhodopsin**, and so can only provide monochrome information. The rods are more sensitive at lower levels of light and to light at the blue end of the spectrum. This is why, in night vision, colours fade and the world takes on the bluish colour of moonlight. In night vision it is also the case that, unlike in daylight conditions, vision is better not in central vision, but in peripheral vision (because there are more rods there). Soldiers are trained to look 'sideways' under conditions of darkness, to improve their chances of detecting objects and movements by making greater use of rods rather than cones.

The sensory changes detected by the rods and cones are converted into neural impulses and passed to **bipolar** cells which interconnect a small number of receptors. Groups of bipolar cells in turn connect to **ganglion** cells. The axons of the ganglion cells are bundled together and pass out of the eye forming the **optic nerve**, which is one of the cranial nerves (figure 2.1). In the periphery of the retina, one ganglion cell might collect information from hundreds of rods, while in central vision, it may receive inputs from only a small number of cones.

Integration and communication across the retina is also accomplished by **horizontal** and **amacrine** cells. The horizontal cells interconnect receptors and bipolar cells across a region of the retina; amacrine cells interconnect bipolar cells and ganglion cells at a higher level (figure 2.1).

There is one very peculiar thing about the retina, and that is that it appears to be built back-to-front. The receptors do not point to the source of the light, but towards the supporting cells at the back of the eye. Before it arrives at the receptors, the light must pass through the layers of retinal cells and the blood vessels inside the eye. There is an explanation for this odd state of affairs in terms of the way in which the eyes of mammals have evolved from the more elementary eyes of amphibians, but it is surprising that such high-quality vision can be achieved despite this apparent biological handicap. You generally cannot be aware of the 'wiring' at the inside of the retina, but you may be aware of the blood vessels. If you see a flash of lightening, or a flash from a stroboscope, you may well get an after-image with a tree-like pattern of lines, which are the shadows of the blood vessels thrown upon the retina by the brief intense flash. If you gaze at an unpatterned bright surface, especially the blue sky, and concentrate on an area to the side of where your gaze is fixed, you will probably be able to see small transparent blobs floating along. What you are seeing are the red blood cells as they pass along the blood vessels inside the eye.

This arrangement of the retina has another consequence. This is that the wiring, once gathered into the optic nerve, must pass out of the eye. There can be no receptors at this point, and so a small area with no vision, the **blind spot**, results. We are normally quite unaware of this gap in our vision, because the brain 'fills in' the missing section with what it thinks should be there. By careful arrangement, however, the system can be fooled into revealing the blind spot. One way of doing this is by using the stimuli in figure 2.2. Close your right eye and hold your head about 17 cm away from the upper cross. Look steadily at the cross, so maintaining it over the fovea. By moving the page to and fro you should easily find a position where the disc to the left completely disappears. Light from the region of the disc will now be focused over the blind spot. Now, keeping in the same position relative to the page, fixate (look at) the lower cross: the gap in the line will be filled in. In the first case, the visual system no longer has any evidence for the disc (although you 'know' it is there) so it disappears. In the second case, there is no evidence for the gap, so the gap disappears.

The optic nerves from the two eyes travel back to a point just in front of the stalk which supports the pituitary gland, where they meet at the **optic chiasm**. Here the nerves which have come from the nasal (inner) halves of each retina cross over. The nerves from the temporal (outer) half-retinas do not cross. In this way, information which has come from one side of visual space, but through both eyes, is gathered together and passed back to the opposite hemisphere of the brain (see figure 2.3).

From the chiasm, the nerve fibres pass back to the **lateral geniculate** nucleus which is part of the thalamus, and then on to the cerebral cortex in the occipital lobe at the very back of the brain. Here they terminate in the **striate cortex**. Information is then passed to the adjacent areas known as

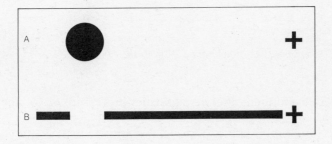

FIGURE 2.2   *Demonstration of the blind spot (see text) (From* Introduction to Psychology, *8th edition, by Rita L. Atkinson, Richard C. Atkinson and Ernest R. Hilgard, copyright © 1983 by Harcourt Brace Jovanovich, Inc. Reprinted by permission of the publisher)*

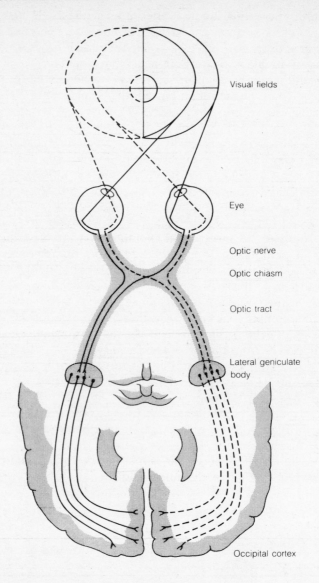

Visual fields

Eye

Optic nerve

Optic chiasm

Optic tract

Lateral geniculate body

Occipital cortex

FIGURE 2.3   *A diagram of the visual pathways from the eye to the cortex*

prestriate cortex and then, after being further processed, on to other areas of the cortex.

There are three important aspects to the arrangement of nerve fibres in the optic tract within the brain. First, the relative spatial position of visual stimuli is maintained by the **topographic** organization of the tract. Although it goes through some distortions, a spatial map of visual space is maintained throughout the system. Secondly, the number of cells in the cortex is related to the acuity of vision. There are more receptors in the fovea than elsewhere in the retina, but an even greater proportion of cortical cells is devoted to receiving information from the receptors in central vision. Thirdly, there are several projections from one part of the lateral geniculate to the cortex. The cortex receives not just a single representation of the sensory information, but a number of different representations processed in different ways and, presumably, used for different purposes.

Finally you should note that, although the system from the optic chiasm through the lateral geniculate to the striate cortex is the **primary visual system** giving high-quality form perception, visual information is passed to other parts of the brain. Some of it is used to control eye movements, and some feeds into the general reticular activating system. Another important element is the **secondary visual system** which passes from the optic tract to other subcortical and midbrain areas, and may be used for spatial localization.

Visual sensory processing

How is information processed within the visual system so that complex visual perception is achieved? Although the system is organized topographically, it is a mistake to think that an image is registered by the retina and then simply passed back to the cortex almost as if it were a photographic slide being projected. It is more the case that the visual stimulation is broken up into all its component aspects, encoded, and then passed up to the cortex where the information is reassembled and interpreted.

One point which emphasizes that the eye is not simply registering images is that it is in continuous motion. Even when we believe that we are looking steadily at some object, the eye is constantly making very small movements called **saccades**. This continually alters the position of the image as it falls upon the retina. One reason why this is useful lies in the nature of stimulus detection. The receptors detect the light by bleaching of the photopigments, which then have to be replaced. If the image was stable, the pigments would have less time to recover in regions of high stimulation. Also, any nervous tissue becomes less responsive with repeated stimulation, and also needs an opportunity to recover (see p. 18). The movement no doubt also helps to reduce the problems of parts of the retina being obscured by blood vessels, by giving an opportunity for slightly different parts of the stimulus to be viewed by different sets of receptors. If the image is held stable with respect to the retina, by linking its movement to the movement of the eye, producing a **stabilized retinal image**, then the image fades and may completely disappear.

The retina is also capable of adapting to different levels of stimulation. One form of **adaptation** is dark-adaptation involving the transfer from cone-vision to rod-vision. You will know how when you enter a dark room almost nothing is visible. After about five minutes, things will be much clearer and improvement in vision will continue for up to half an hour. Adaptation back to daylight conditions is much more rapid.

There is also **local adaptation** in the retina. You may be aware how difficult it is to photograph a television screen in a normally lit room. Either the television or the room will be properly exposed, but not both. However, you can easily see the television screen and the surrounding room because the eye can adjust different regions of the retina to be sensitive to whatever falls in that region.

Peripheral analysis   The retina is active in other ways. One of the advantages of having cells which interconnect adjacent receptors is that the cells can interact with each other. A clear example occurs in **lateral inhibition**. If a given receptor is active, it affects the action of an adjacent cell. If there is a difference in the intensity of stimulation falling on the two cells, this will tend to increase the apparent difference, as the brighter will be less affected by the less bright. This has the effect of 'sharpening-up' contours (edges) as they fall on the retina. The effect of this process can be seen in the stimulus array shown in figure 2.4 which has been called the Hermann Grid. If you gaze at this image, you should note something unusual: grey blobs seem to appear at the intersection of the white lines, especially outside the central area of fixation. This visual illusion can be explained by lateral inhibition. Consider a point on one of the white lines next to the middle of a square. This is surrounded by quite a lot of black, so there will be a large effect of lateral inhibition, making the white seem whiter. Now consider a point in the middle of one of the intersections. This is immediately next to much less black, so there will be less effect, and the white will seem less white – hence the apparent grey blobs.

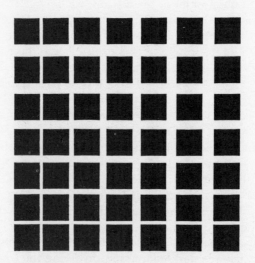

FIGURE 2.4   *An illustration of lateral inhibition (see text)*

Intensity, pattern and movement The retina also actively analyses the features of the stimulation, encodes the result of this analysis and passes the encoded information back to the cortex. There are at least three different kinds of ganglion cell in the retina which together are able to provide this information. Each kind has a **receptive field** of receptors. One kind of cell (**on-centre**) is more neurally active when light falls in the centre of the receptive field, but is less active than usual when light falls on the edge of the receptor field. The opposite is the case with **off-centre** cells. The third kind, **transient** cells, have larger receptive fields and seem to respond to movements, particularly if they are sudden. The output from these ganglion cells is integrated in complex ways so that the eye is able to transmit information about **intensity** (or brightness), **pattern** and **movement**, as well as other features.

A related form of analysis takes place in the cerebral striate cortex. Hubel and Wiesel recorded the activity of single cells in the cortex of cats and found that different cells responded to different kinds of visual stimulation (Hubel and Wiesel, 1962). They identified three different types of cortical cell. **Simple** cells responded to a simple bar of light presented to the animal in a particular orientation in the appropriate receptive field of the cell. Change the angle, and the response diminished. Different cells responded to different angles. **Complex** cells had larger receptive fields, and were maximally responsive to a bar shown at a given angle, but only when it was moved to and fro. **Hypercomplex** cells (which are more common in prestriate cortex) responded not only to a moving bar at a given angle, but when it was of a specific length.

The perception of intensity or brightness is therefore principally encoded in the retina by the pattern and level of activity in the on-centre and off-centre cells. Certain information, in the form of contours and perhaps specific features, which will subsequently be analysed at the level of the cortex to provide pattern and shape perception, is also encoded in the retina. The combined activity of cells responding to light at the centre (on-centre) or at the edge (off-centre) of their receptive fields provides a clear definition of contours (or 'edges') where there are sudden changes in brightness. These contours are essential in defining the shape of objects which will be perceived. At the level of the cortex, the information about intensity and contours is further processed by the simple, complex and hypercomplex cells to reveal the shape and orientation of the contours and areas of brightness, and the presence of particular features such as corners and angles. From this is built up the perceptual description of the shapes, patterns and textures which are being seen.

Movement is detected at the level of the cortex by the complex and hypercomplex cells. As the visual scene is in continual motion across the retina as a result of eye movements, the effects of the motion which is solely due to the eyes moving must be subtracted to reveal the 'real' motion in the external world. (You can trick the system by gently pushing your eyeball from the side. This movement cannot be attributed to internally generated eye movements and so the visual world appears to move to and fro.) The apparent movement of contours and features must be related to the systems detecting shape and pattern in order to deduce the relative movements of specific objects. These must in turn also be related to perceived movement of the self in external space so that the visual world is seen as stable as we move about in it. This involves a considerable degree of co-operation and integration among different systems within the cortex.

It is clear, not only that the retina is active in analysing the features of visual stimulation, but also that a considerable degree of processing of visual sensation takes place at higher levels. There may well be feature detectors in the cortex not only for orientation, movement and length of visual components, but also for particular shapes, sizes and objects. All this basic information about the component characteristics of the stimulation must be re-combined to build up a total picture of the visual environment in the form of meaningful perceptions.

Colour   The processing of colour is carried out by a system which runs side-by-side with the systems for intensity, pattern and movement. The first stage in this system is the response of the cones in the retina. There are three types of cone which respond most actively to light at different wavelengths (Marks et al., 1964). One type is most responsive to blue light at around 445 nanometres (blue-sensitive), another type to green light at around 535 nm (green-sensitive) and a third responsive to light at around 570 nm which is yellow (although the cones are termed red-sensitive). There is, of course, considerable overlap in the response curves of these cones as figure 2.5 shows. This is a **trichromatic** process because the colour of the light is analysed in terms of how much blue, green and red light it contains.

While the retina encodes colour in terms of three constituent components, the output through the ganglion cells and on to the lateral geniculate becomes re-coded in a different way. Coding at this level is in terms of **opponent processes** (DeValois et al., 1966). Cells in the lateral geniculate seem to be of four kinds: those which increase their activity to red light but decrease with green (R+G−), those increasing to green and decreasing to red (G+R−), those increasing to blue but decreasing to yellow (B+Y−), and those cells which increase to yellow light but decrease to blue (Y+B−). There are also cells which simply respond to black and white. Some of the cells in the lateral geniculate appear to be associated with particular receptive fields.

The coding of colour in the cortex is much less certain. There is evidence that some cortical cells are responsive to opponent processes and some responsive to the three trichromatic categories. The analysis of sensation at the cortex is complex and it is probable that both types of processing are involved.

It is interesting that for many years there was an active debate between those who supported a trichromatic theory of colour vision as originally proposed by Young in 1801 and later modified by Helmholtz, and those who

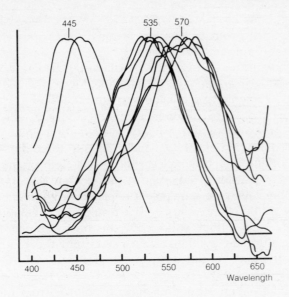

FIGURE 2.5 *The responses of various cones to different wavelengths of light, showing that they can be grouped into three types (From Marks et al. 1964, copyright 1964 by the AAAS)*

supported the opponent process theory developed by Hering in 1878. Both theories have turned out to be partly correct.

One powerful piece of evidence for the trichromatic theory is that it is possible to generate white light by mixing light of the three colours: blue, green and red. The full range of colours can be created by mixing these colours in appropriate combinations (although remember that we are mixing coloured *light*, and not mixing pigments where the primary colours are red, yellow and blue). Colour television pictures are created by combining pictures generated in each of the three colours.

On the other hand, two pieces of evidence support the opponent process theory. One is the after-images which can be seen after prolonged stimulation by a given colour. If you gaze steadily at a large patch of red light for about a minute, and then shift your gaze to a blank white area, you will see an after-image of the opponent colour: green. If you gaze at a green patch, then the after-image will be red. The same effect can be seen for the pair blue–yellow. What happens is that prolonged stimulation leads to the system becoming less responsive to the colour being fixated. On shifting fixation, it takes the system time to recover. In the interim, the system is more responsive to the opposite colour, and so that colour will be apparent in the white light as it dominates its opponent partner.

The second piece of evidence concerns colour-blindness. Those with normal colour vision are termed **trichromats** because they see all three combinations of red–green, blue–yellow and black–white. Some individuals, however, are unable to see the difference between red and green, or between blue and yellow. Having only two of the combinations operating, they are known as **dichromats**. The loss of red–green colour vision is much the more common form, and afflicts about 1 in 15 men and 1 in 100 women (the sex difference results from genetic sex-linking). In rare cases only one combination, the perception of black–white, is preserved and these **monochromats** are unable to see colours at all.

We now know that these different forms of evidence reflect activity in different parts or levels of the sensory system for colour. This system produces a final sensation of colour which varies in three dimensions: hue, saturation and brightness. **Hue** reflects the wavelength of the light and is usually reflected in its name: red, yellow, orange, and so on. **Saturation** is the strength of the colour, or how pale it appears. **Brightness** is determined by the intensity of the energy source. The resulting combination of colours can be arranged in a **colour solid** with the hues arranged around the circumference, saturation by the distance out from the central axis, and brightness by variations up and down the central axis.

Depth   **Depth** information – how far away a point is from the observer – also involves various levels in the visual sensory system. This is because a number of elements are combined in the perception of depth. Some of these elements can be sensed using only one eye, but others rely upon the use of both eyes. Using only one eye, there are three main ways in which we can derive depth information. One is aerial **haze**, the fact that objects further away appear lighter, and the colours less saturated, than those closer to. A second is the use of **texture gradients**: regular patterns become less definite, and the elements closer together, as they are further away, as in figure 2.6 (Gibson, 1950).

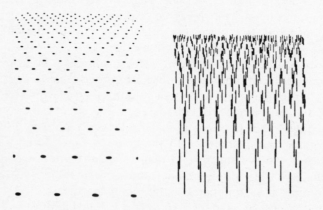

FIGURE 2.6   *Two examples of texture gradients (From Taylor et al., 1982)*

Thirdly, there is **interposition**, the fact that nearer objects tend to partly obscure those which are further away. Associated with interposition is **motion parallax**: the fact that as we move about the relative motion of objects gives us clues about their distance. As we move (watch from a car or train) distant objects seem to move with us, and nearer objects appear to move in a direction opposite to our own movement. The nearer they are, the faster objects seem move.

However, using only a single eye, our depth vision is limited. Using two eyes, it is very much better because we can make use of **retinal disparity**. If you alternately close one eye and then the other, you will see that each eye has a slightly different view of the world. The nearer an object, the larger the apparent shift as you switch eyes, and the larger the retinal disparity. The brain makes use of this information to determine the depth of objects and there is evidence that there are special cells in the cortex (disparity detectors) which respond specifically to this information (Barlow et al., 1967).

The sensory visual systems which we have considered so far all concern the primary visual system which runs through the lateral geniculate to the cortex (see p. 40). It is interesting that if areas in the striate visual cortex are electrically stimulated while the brain is exposed during an operation (there are no sensory receptors in the brain, so the patient does not feel the stimulus being applied) then the patient will report that brief flashes of light are seen and will be able to point to where they appear to be. If some of the surrounding cortical areas are stimulated, then the patient may report more meaningful visual experiences, describing objects and even complex scenes which may well be coloured and in motion.

Some attempts have been made to rehabilitate patients, in whom the optic tract is damaged but the visual cortex is intact, by directly stimulating the cortex (Rushton and Brindley, 1977). A camera mounted upon the head points to the scene in front of the patient and relays images to a computer which then stimulates the surface of the brain at appropriate points through a matrix of tiny electrodes placed beneath the skull. This system attempts to simulate the activity of the eye and optic tract and so replace them, with the eventual aim of fully restoring normal vision. In this way a crude version of an image can already be generated in the brain, although the procedure is still a long way from reconstituting normal vision.

Other attempts at rehabilitation have been made for those in whom the cortex has been seriously damaged, although the eye and optic nerve are intact. Although these patients have no experience of sight, and say that they are blind, it has been shown that they are able to locate objects and also make some simple discriminations – between 'O's and 'X's, for example. No visual experience goes with this, and the patients feel as if they were just guessing. The phenomenon is known as **blindsight** (Campion et al., 1983). It is believed that it may in part result from the operation of the more primitive subcortical secondary visual system which may still play a role in normal spatial localization. However, although the blind patients retain this ability, it is proving extremely difficult to assist them to make use of the 'sight' which they retain.

Visual perception

The encoding of visual stimulation and its transmission to the cortex is only the first stage in our understanding of the visual world around us. The sensory information has to be interpreted and made meaningful – it must be converted into **percepts**.

When we perceive objects, we do not perceive them in terms of the separately encoded elements, but in terms of *whole* objects. The importance of the way in which perception is organized into **holistic** patterns was first recognized by the **Gestalt** psychologists in the early part of this century (*Gestalt* is a German word meaning 'form' or 'configuration'). Among the principles of perceptual organization which the Gestalt psychologists described are perceptual grouping and figure–ground relationships.

Perceptual **grouping** reflects the tendency to see ordered structures in the visual patterns we observe. For instance, the upper part of figure 2.7 will be seen as three columns of three discs, while the lower part will appear to be three rows of three discs. This is a powerful effect and it is difficult to 'see' the figures in any other way.

Figure–ground relationships also relate to our attempts to structure the world. Given a simple outline, we tend to see it as a boundary which indicates a figure placed against a ground behind it. In a simplified and ambiguous case, as in figure 2.8, it is possible to see either a vase against a dark background, or else two heads facing each other in silhouette against a mainly white background. There is insufficient information for the mind to

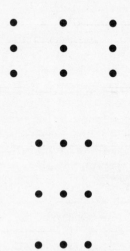

FIGURE 2.7   *Gestalt organization. The upper figure appears as three columns, the lower as three rows*

decide which is the correct interpretation, and if you gaze at the figure it will appear to **reverse** between the two possibilities. Most situations are not ambiguous and we correctly identify the figure and the ground.

Another general principle of perception is **constancy**. Although objects appear to us in a variety of spatial transformations, we are able to identify the object as being the 'same'. The cup in figure 2.9 may appear in the orientations shown, but it is still seen as being a cup. Constancy applied not only to shape but also to size. The actual size, as projected upon the retina, of a friend increases as she or he moves towards us. However, we do not see our friend as growing taller – we see a person of a fixed height moving nearer.

There are other constancies for colour, lightness and location. If a banana is seen under blue light, it will still appear yellow. It is only if most of the scene is blanked out (by viewing through a small key hole) so that it cannot be seen what the object is, that it will appear blue. Similarly, even under intense white light, black velvet appears black. However, blank out most of the scene, so that only a small patch on the surface is seen, and it will appear white.

Location constancy enables us to see a stable world. As we move about, the image of the visual world is constantly shifting. However, we do not *see* the world as unstable. We are able to attribute the relative motion to the movement of our own eyes and bodies in space. The mind can then cancel out the effect of this movement so as to enable us to see an apparently stable visual scene.

Perception is, however, more than principles of organization and the operation of constancies. In recent years cognitive psychologists have emphasized that perception is an **active** process (Gregory, 1977). We reason

FIGURE 2.8 *An ambiguous figure which may appear as a vase or two faces, depending on which is seen as a figure and which as ground (From* Introduction to Psychology, *8th edition, by Rita L. Atkinson, Richard C. Atkinson and Ernest R. Hilgard, copyright © 1983 by Harcourt Brace Jovanovich, Inc. Reprinted by permission of the publisher)*

FIGURE 2.9 *Shape constancy. Although its appearance varies, it is still seen as the same cup (After Lefrancois, 1980)*

about the world and on the basis of our past experience have expectations about the world and the objects which we expect to see in it. Faced with incoming sensory data, we construct **hypotheses** about what it is that we might perceive and then test out these hypotheses using the available data.

Most of the time our hypotheses are correct and lead us to respond appropriately. However, particularly if the information is ambiguous, we can either be left uncertain about the correct interpretation or else be led to absurd conclusions. In figure 2.10 the Necker cube is ambiguous and can be seen as a cube from above and to the right, or else from below and to the left. If you gaze at it it will repeatedly reverse between these possibilities. The mind constructs two alternative hypotheses, but cannot find the evidence to choose between them. In the case of the Devil's tuning-fork, each of the elements of the figure make sense with respect to the adjacent parts, so acceptable hypotheses are generated. However, it is only when the

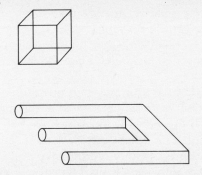

FIGURE 2.10   *Two ambiguous figures: the Necker cube and the Devil's tuning-fork*

whole is considered that it is seen as an **impossible figure**. It certainly 'looks all right', until you consider how you might try to make it.

The context is also important in determining perception. In the upper row of figure 2.11 the central item appears to be 'B', although when the same item appears in the lower row, it appears to be '13'. Similarly, a circle drawn on white paper accompanied by the word 'ball' will be seen differently from a circle next to the word 'hole'.

Experience plays an important part in the hypotheses we construct. Another interesting example comes from studies of eye-witness testimony (Loftus et al., 1978). Although not all blond people have blue eyes, it is more common. A recognized error in witnesses giving descriptions is to incorrectly report that the suspect's eyes were blue, when only the blond hair has been clearly perceived. This error is caused by our tendency to see what we expect to see, in line with making sense of our visual world. Generally, the way in which the mind fills in missing detail can be useful, but occasionally it can lead us to make quite serious errors of judgement.

Happily, not all of these errors are serious, and those provided by **visual illusions** are intriguing and entertaining. They are also of scientific interest because analysis of the mistakes which the visual system makes can reveal the nature of the underlying processes. We have already seen in figure 2.4 how an illusion can result from the process of lateral inhibition. However, not only processes at the retinal level, but at all levels through the sensory system, are associated with various illusions. A selection of the geometric illusions is shown in figure 2.12. Not all of these are fully understood, but the way in which elements of the stimulus are encoded, mutual interference

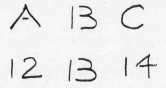

FIGURE 2.11   *The effect of context on whether the central item appears as 'B' or '13'*

among stimulus elements, selective feature detection, prior experience and purely cognitive factors, can all be shown to play some part in generating these illusions. It is also interesting that knowing about the illusion, and even understanding how it is created, does not lessen the power of the illusory effect.

It may be surprising that we do not apparently suffer from the effects of these illusions very often in everyday life. Most of the time we do not notice any discrepancy between the visual world which we perceive and the world which we detect through our other senses. This is no doubt because in everyday living there is a great deal of **redundancy** in the visual information we receive. There is more information than we strictly need for perception. There are usually a variety of **cues** (prompts) to guide our perception, and in putting these together we no doubt avoid the errors that might result from using one clue alone. We also combine visual information with information from other senses, notably touch and hearing, so that an accurate mental representation of the external world can be built up and give us the vivid perceptual experiences we enjoy. (An experiment showing how subjective contours can generate apparent depth is presented in box 2.1.)

The Auditory System

Structure of the auditory system

When we hear sounds we are detecting changes in air pressure as they occur at the ear. These changes in air pressure have a cyclical pattern and move in a wavelike fashion. We can therefore consider sounds (pure **tones**) as having a **frequency**, which is the number of cycles in a unit time, and an **intensity**, which is the amplitude of the wave or the size of the regular changes. Real sounds are, of course, complex and are made up of many components with different frequencies and intensities, but we can consider them as made up of a collection of pure tones.

The sound waves arrive at the **external ear** and enter the **auditory canal**, which are the parts of the ear which are normally visible. At the end of the auditory canal is the **ear-drum** or **tympanic membrane** (see figure 2.13) which is deflected so that it moves with the same frequency as the sound waves.

Beyond the ear-drum is the **middle ear** which contains three small bones (ossicles). The **malleus** ('hammer') is linked to the ear-drum and transmits its movement to the **incus** ('anvil') which in turn passes the vibrations on to the **stapes** ('stirrup') and so on to the inner ear. A tube passes from the middle ear to the top of the throat and allows some compensation for marked changes in external air pressure. When your ears 'pop' while gaining or losing altitude, this is the result of the tube opening at the end where it reaches the throat.

The **inner ear** therefore receives the transmitted pattern of sound waves,

Are the white blocks rectangular?

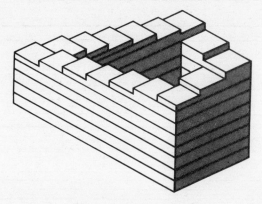

Where do the stairs lead?

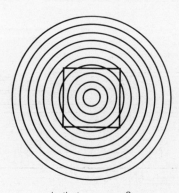

Is that a square?

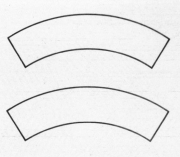

Are the curves equal?

continued

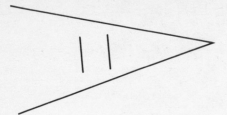

Are the two verticals
the same length?

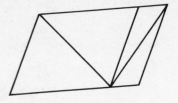

Are the diagonals the
same length?

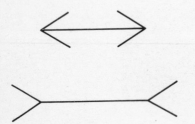

Are the horizontal lines
the same length?

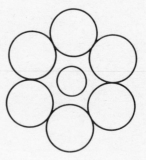

Are the centre circles
the same size?

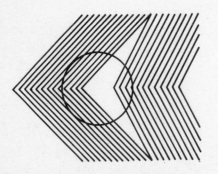

Is that a circle?

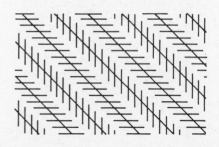

Are the diagonals parallel?

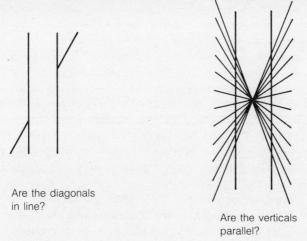

Are the diagonals
in line?

Are the verticals
parallel?

FIGURE 2.12 *A selection of geometrical visual illusions (From Robinson, 1972)*

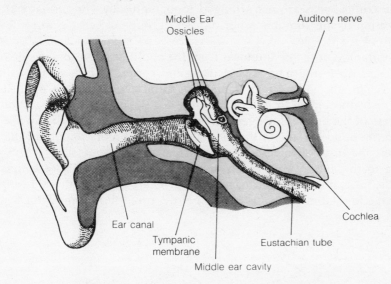

Middle Ear
Ossicles

Auditory nerve

Cochlea

Ear canal

Tympanic
membrane

Middle ear cavity

Eustachian tube

FIGURE 2.13 *A diagrammatic section through the right ear (After Munn, 1966)*

and contains the sensory receptors for the detection of the sound (and also
for balance and position sense). The auditory receptors are contained in a
fluid-filled structure, the **cochlea**. The cochlea is really like a long tube
which has been coiled up until it looks rather like a snail-shell (figure 2.14).
It is really like one tube contained within another tube. The stirrup of the
middle ear rests against the **oval window** which is at one end of the outer
tube. Pressure waves are set up inside the cochlea and transmitted to the
basilar membrane, moving the **hair cells** of the **organ of Corti** which are
attached to it. These are forced against the more rigid **tectorial membrane**

above. Neural potentials are created in the hair cells which pass to ganglion cells and on to the **auditory** (or cochlear) **nerve**. This is not unlike the chain of connections from retinal receptors to the optic nerve.

When the pressure waves are transmitted to the basilar membrane, a standing wave is created. The whole membrane does not vibrate equally, but one part vibrates much more strongly than the rest. Which part vibrates most strongly depends upon the frequency of the original sound wave. High frequencies vibrate the end of the basilar membrane nearer to the middle ear, low frequencies the part further away (von Békésy, 1960). It is in this way that frequency can be detected. However, the precise mechanism by which the hair cells generate neural potentials is still poorly understood (Masterson, 1974)

From the auditory nerve, which is the eighth cranial nerve, impulses pass up to the **medial geniculate** body of the thalamus and then on to the cortex, arriving at the upper part of the temporal lobe (to be discussed more fully in chapter 3). This is the primary centre in the cortex for hearing. Unlike vision, the cortical cells are not arranged topographically – in terms of the spatial location of the stimulus – but different groups of cells seem to deal with different frequencies.

It is important to note that impulses from the auditory nerve at one side of the head pass up to the medial geniculate and cortex on *both* sides of the brain. In vision, the visual field at one side projects only to the opposite hemisphere of the brain. In audition, sensation at one ear passes to both hemispheres of the brain. However, it is still the case that the pathway from one ear to the opposite side of the brain is larger and more important than the one passing to the hemisphere of the brain on the same side.

Damage to the auditory nerve on one side of the head will, of course, produce deafness in the ear on that side. However, deafness rarely results from damage to the brain. This is because of the projection from each ear to

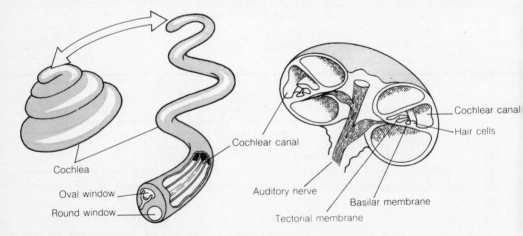

FIGURE 2.14   *The cochlea and its internal structure (After Munn, 1966)*

both sides of the brain (bilateral projection). For auditory functions to be completely destroyed, the auditory areas on both sides of the brain would have to be damaged and this is rare in patients who survive their injuries. More common are injuries which affect only one side of the brain. These may alter hearing thresholds or distort the perception of sounds, but do not produce complete deafness.

Artificial stimulation of the auditory areas of the cortex, exposed at surgery, will result in the patient reporting that he or she hears single tones. However, stimulation of the surrounding areas will result in reports of meaningful sounds ('a door slamming', 'a tap running') or even of complete melodies being heard. Again, this is similar to the organization found for vision.

Auditory sensory processing

There appear to be four main aspects to the sensory experience of sound: pitch (frequency), loudness (intensity), timbre and location (localization). These aspects are coded and analysed by different processes in the auditory information-processing system.

Pitch Frequency, or **pitch** as it becomes as a sensory quality, is as you now know encoded by the vibration of different sites on the basilar membrane. Throughout the auditory system there seem to be neural cells which respond most actively to stimulation of a given frequency. In this way, the information that a given frequency is present can be passed fairly directly to the cortex. However, although most cells respond maximally to a given frequency, they also respond to some degree to adjacent higher and lower frequencies. Some cells respond over quite a broad range. There is also a curious absence of cells which respond to frequencies in the lower range of hearing, although there is good discrimination of pitch at this level. It is thought that an additional method of coding, employing temporal patterns of stimuli in which some nerves fire on every cycle of the stimulus wave and some nerves fire more intermittently, may be used to give sensation of these lower frequencies (Uttal, 1973).

Loudness Intensity of the stimulation, or **loudness** as it becomes as a sensation, is coded in a more complex way. Loudness is not coded independently of frequency, so that the response of a given cell in the auditory pathway will differ for two tones, even if they are of the same loudness. There seem to be insufficient neurons to separately encode all the levels of loudness we can detect at each frequency, and so the coding of loudness must involve the combined activities of a number of cells. There seem to be some cells which increase their activity with increasing loudness, others which decrease their activity with increases in loudness, and yet others which show various patterns of increase and decrease. Presumably this information can be combined in the brain to give us accurate sensory information about sound intensity. Our perception of intensity is relatively accurate, although it does vary somewhat with pitch: for two sounds of different pitches to sound equally loud, they may well not be of exactly equal physical intensity.

Timbre   The third sensory dimension which we hear is **timbre** or the quality of the sound. The same note produced on a euphonium and on a trombone sounds different. This is because we do not, in general, hear pure tones but tones made up of a **fundamental** accompanied by a range of harmonics and overtones (figure 2.15). In everyday life we hear **complex** sounds which are made up of a bundle of different frequencies. In the case of the euphonium and the trombone the fundamental frequency is the same, so that it is the 'same' note, but the associated frequencies are different.

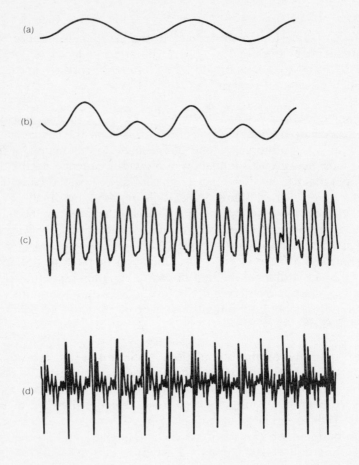

FIGURE 2.15   *The physical nature of sounds: (a) a fundamental (pure tone), (b) a fundamental with second harmonic, (c) complex sound: a euphonium playing B$_b$, (d) complex sound: a tenor trombone playing B$_b$*

The timbre may be partly encoded in the auditory system because there is some evidence for cells in the auditory cortex which only respond to complex sounds. Some of these cells may be responding to sounds which have particular biological importance – alarm calls or distress signals from other animals of the same species, perhaps. However, the existence of such cells has not been clearly shown in humans. At least part of the sensation of timbre must come from processes in the brain which follow the reception of information about the component frequencies. One pattern will be analysed as being typical of a euphonium, another pattern as typical of a trombone. This processing presumably occurs in the cortex in the regions surrounding the primary areas for sound reception.

Location   Finally, we are able to locate sounds in space with reasonable accuracy. As with depth information in vision, there is more than one cue to sound **localization**. There are in fact two main methods employed and both rely upon our having two ears. The first is based upon **phase differences**. The pressure waves originating from the sound source are likely to arrive at the two ears at a different phase in their cycles. At a given moment the wave arriving at the left ear may be going up, while the wave at the right ear may be going down. As there are cells which respond at particular phases in the cycle of the stimulating wave, these phase differences can be detected by cells higher up in the auditory system. Unless the sound source is directly in front of or behind the individual, some pattern of phase differences will be generated by any complex sound, and the phase difference detectors will analyse this pattern and calculate the position source of the sound.

There are not only phase differences but also **intensity differences** at the two ears. Unless the sound source is equidistant from the two ears, the intensity of sound will be greater at the ear nearer to the sound source. Again, these differences in loudness can be analysed by the system and the position of the sound source determined. It is possible to generate the illusion of a sound having a particular source by artificially manipulating the phase and intensity relationships of the stimuli presented at the two ears. You may well have tried stereo headphones with volume controls on each earpiece. Given a fairly simple stimulus, increasing the relative loudness at one ear will make the sound appear to shift towards that side of space. The same effect can be produced to some extent by altering the balance control on a stereo system. Understanding how sound localization is achieved can also make it clear why we can sometimes find it difficult to decide if a sound is in front of or behind us, especially if it is near the midline and there are no visual cues as to its location.

Auditory perception

Auditory perception is much less well understood than visual perception. This is partly because we do not have a good theory of how sounds are perceived when they are mixed. Sounds are analysed in terms of pitch, loudness and timbre rather in the same way that colours are analysed in terms of hue, brightness and saturation. However, although we have a good understanding of how colours may be mixed (not only scientifically – a primary school child soon learns how to mix colours for painting), it is much more difficult to describe the effects of mixing two tones together.

Sound in which all frequencies are equally present is known as **white noise** and sounds rather like a bathroom shower or a television not tuned into any channel. In a way, this is rather like white light, in which all colours are present. However, mixtures of specific sets of pure tones can have effects which are difficult to predict.

One reason is that cognitive factors, especially previous experience and cultural learning, play an important part in how we perceive sounds. It will be obvious that Westerners find much Eastern music apparently discordant and unpleasant, at least without a period of learning how to appreciate it. This music sounds perfectly consonant to Eastern listeners. The difference is simply exposure during childhood, together with expectations which have been learned about how good music 'ought to sound'. The context also plays a role, just as it does in vision.

In general, tones which are closer together are more likely to be considered discordant than are tones which are further apart. However, if the tones are very close together, they may not be heard as separate pitches, but as the (consonant or dissonant) overtones of a single sound. The whole situation is further complicated by the fact that the mind may fill in a **missing fundamental** sound. Presented with a set of harmonic overtones which are normally associated with a given fundamental pitch, the hearer may perceive that the fundamental tone is actually present (Roederer, 1975).

A final way in which auditory perception differs from visual perception is the relative importance of the temporal patterning of the sensations. As vision is spatially organized, it is possible to perceive different elements in the visual field at the same time. This is much less true of hearing. We can appreciate different sounds originating from different sources at the same time, but it is very much more difficult to do. It is not part of the normal experience of sound, at least for humans. As a result, the temporal organization of sound takes on a greater importance. We are aware of how sounds change, how the changes often imply movement of the sound source, and especially of how there are temporal patterns in the sounds. We are quick to perceive regular **rhythms** in the sounds that we hear, and they are an important aspect of auditory experience.

The encoding of sensation as carried out by the auditory system, and the cognitive interpretation and perception of that sensation are not the only important factors in determining what we hear. **Attention** also plays a part. We do not perceive all the sounds (or the visual stimuli) which fall upon our sensory receptors. By attentional mechanisms certain sounds are filtered out for further sensory processing. At a later stage there is further selection so that just a few sounds will enter conscious awareness. It is obvious that much of the stimulation is processed to some extent within the system, but without our being aware of it unless it is of sufficient psychological importance. You will probably have experienced the 'cocktail party phenomenon' in which, while surrounded by all sorts of conversations and incidental noises to which you are not listening, you will suddenly hear your name spoken on the other side of the room. Your name intrudes into the conversation you are concentrating on and distracts you.

This illustrates two aspects of attention. First, it illustrates that you can actively select what to attend to. In a noisy room you can concentrate on just the conversation you are holding. While attending to it, you will only be aware of that conversation in any detail. Questioned later about events at the party, you will probably only recall that conversation and not the others around you. Secondly, it illustrates that a certain amount of passive processing occurs for the sounds which are not normally being heard. Those sounds of some significance – your name, a fire-alarm, running water – will be detected and result in an intrusion into awareness.

One way in which auditory attention can be studied is by the **dichotic listening** technique. This was mentioned in chapter 1, and will be discussed further in chapter 3, as a technique for investigating lateral asymmetry of organization in the brain. It can also be used as a way of presenting two different **channels** of information to the individual, by playing different audio recordings to the left and right ears. The subject can be instructed to listen to, and remember, what is being presented to one of the ears. The subject can then subsequently be tested to see how much of the attended and unattended messages can be recalled. Alternatively, the subject may be asked to **shadow** the message at one ear by repeating aloud what is heard. Intrusions from the unattended channel (ear) can be recorded besides subsequent recall being examined (Treisman et al., 1974).

Dichotic studies show that, in general, only physical characteristics from the unattended channel will be subsequently recalled, especially if the task is demanding, as when the subject is asked to shadow. The subject will be aware of the sex of the speaker at the unattended channel (high or low pitched voice), or if speech changes to music or other non-speech sounds. A change of language may also be detected because of the different characteristics of the speech sounds. Only the content of the message from the *attended* ear will be subsequently recalled, unless there is some special reason for the material at the unattended ear to intrude.

These attentional processes apply to all sensory modalities, but they have been most studied in auditory perception, partly because auditory stimuli can be more easily controlled in the laboratory.

Speech perception

The perception of speech and language is a particular aspect of auditory perception of special interest to psycholinguists and cognitive psychologists. Even the perception of single words turns out to be quite a feat, without the added complexities of interpreting the meaning of the words when they are built up to form sentences in a given language. How remarkable is this human achievement is shown by how difficult it is proving to be to design computer systems capable of 'natural language understanding'.

In listening to spoken words, there is often a marked difference between the physical stimulation arriving at the senses and the sounds which we actually hear. We perceive (hear) a string of quite distinct words. However, examination of the physical pattern of stimulation can show that there are all sorts of brief pauses and gaps in the sound energy *within* words, which are sometimes much larger than the gaps *between* words. There is also a mismatch between the pattern of sound and what we hear. The same physical sound, but placed in different contexts (perhaps as part of different words or embedded in different sentences), can sound to the hearer as quite different. On the other hand, some quite dramatic differences in physical stimulation can be completely undetected in certain contexts. This is because of the effect of subsequent cognitive perceptual processing.

It is still poorly understood how we identify the component speech sounds which make up words: **phonemes**. In the words 'bed' and 'bet' the 'b' and 'e' components sound just the same. However, because the vocal tract is preparing to form the final consonant, both components (and especially the vowel) will differ between the two words. The effect of each phoneme will be influenced by those around it, even if the hearer cannot detect these differences. The problem for the speech-processing system is not to split the word up into phonemes and then identify each one, rather like a child spelling out a word as it is read, but to disentangle the phonemes out of the context in which they are embedded. This is a much more difficult task (Liberman et al., 1967).

Further variations are provided by accents, by differences in the quality of the voice (sex of speaker, telephone transmission, the speaker having a cold), and by differences between languages. Western languages by and large only use inflection for indicating emphasis and questions. In certain other languages, Chinese or Thai, for example, linguistic **tone** is used to distinguish between the meanings of words.

Speech is finally only understood in a full linguistic context. It is very much easier to hear words arranged into meaningful sentences than words produced randomly and in meaningless strings. (Try listening to random strings of words over the telephone: they can be very difficult to hear.) Similarly, words which are unexpected in spoken language, and so difficult for the system to predict or guess at, are harder to hear and are more likely to be misperceived. You are more likely to have to ask someone to repeat their name when they introduce themselves to you, than to ask them what else they said, which is likely to be 'Hello, my name is . . .'. We make use of the considerable **redundancy** of language to help us make sense of what we hear – in terms of individual phonemes, whole words, or strings of words. There is a considerable *cognitive* contribution to the understanding of speech and language, which transforms the sensory stimuli which we receive and processes them to the point where we can extract meaning from them. The same principles apply to all the sensory modalities, but especially in the sophisticated and abstract achievement of understanding language, it is clear how far cognitive processes in perception go beyond the simple interpretation of sensory experiences.

Further reading

A lively introduction, treating the subject in greater detail than is possible here, is S. Coren, C. Porac and L. M. Ward (1979), *Sensation and Perception*, New York: Academic Press.

An entertaining and well-illustrated introduction to the various aspects of visual perception is R. L. Gregory (1977), *Eye and Brain*, (3rd edn), London: World University Library. For cognitive aspects of perception, a well-established and influential text is P. H. Lindsay and D. A. Norman (1977), *Human Information Processing* (2nd edn), New York: Academic Press. It includes more advanced topics such as pattern recognition and forms of internal representation. Another slightly more advanced text is J. M. Wilding (1982), *Perception: From Sense to Object*, London: Hutchinson. This illustrates the contemporary information-processing approach to perception as an interaction between sensation and cognition.

Discussion points

1 Contrast your experiences of daylight and night-time vision. What do the differences tell you about the function of the visual system?

2 How do artists create the illusion of three-dimensional space on a two-dimensional surface? Can you relate this to how the brain interprets depth from visual sensory information?

3 Can you suggest which aspects of the system for processing visual information might be involved in the geometric illusions shown in figure 2.12? (hint – most aspects are involved in one or another illusion and you might consider: lateral inhibition, the effect of spatial organization, possible errors in judging angles, size constancy, perceived depth and cognitive factors.)

4 Describe some situations from your own experience where auditory sensation aids visual perception, and vice versa.

5 Describe the experiences of (a) focusing attention while concentrating hard and (b) attending less actively while daydreaming. How do they differ, and what effects are there on the perception of other stimuli and other modalities (senses)? How does this relate to *conscious* experience?

Practical exercises

1 Examine the effect of context on a well-known ambiguous figure: the 'Wife and Mother-in-Law' illusion (figure 2A).

FIGURE 2A   *The 'Wife and Mother-in-Law' ambiguous figure*

This figure will, on prolonged inspection, alternate between the image of a young woman wearing a choker with her head turned away and the image of an old woman with a large nose wearing a thick fur collar, with her rather pointed chin tucked well down into it. It is always interesting to note which version is the one *first* seen by a subject – presumably the one which the brain finds more probable. About two out of three subjects report seeing the young woman first.

You could check this by showing the figure to a sample of subjects and asking them to describe what they see. You could also time how long it takes before the first 'reversal' occurs.

You could also examine the effect of context by showing a series of other drawings, which are not ambiguous, before the test figure. In one condition they can be young women and in another condition elderly women. Again, record which alternative the subjects report first, and how long it is before they report a reversal.

Does the context have an effect? Do subjects who have seen, say, young women report a young woman in the test figure more commonly? Also, does it take longer for a reversal to occur if a context has been previously set?

2 Determine whether it is more difficult to tell whether sounds are in front of, or behind, a subject rather than to the left or right. Find a quiet room, and preferably one which is fairly plain and symmetrical to left and right as the subject is placed. Find some means of producing a sound which will not vary in pitch, loudness, duration and quality. It should not be too loud. The bleep from a digital watch might be a good choice.

Blindfold the subject and then present the sound a number of times at the four locations: left, right, in front and behind, equidistant from the subject. Try not to give any extra clues by moving about the room noisily. If you can get together with some others who will present the stimuli – so much the better. The locations should occur in a random order (use tables, or shuffle a pack of cards and use the suits to indicate position). The more trials the better. Record the subject's estimates of the position of the tone. Then calculate the accuracy at each position.

You can repeat the experiment with a number of subjects, and it is possible to use more locations, and also different tones. *Is* it harder to discriminate between in front and behind? Does the effect differ for different tones? Does the loudness or pitch of the stimulus make a difference?

(See R. W. Bohlander (1984), Eye position and visual attention influence perceived auditory direction, *Perceptual and Motor Skills*, 59, 483–510.)

3 Conduct a simple shadowing experiment. Use a stereo tape recorder, but record two different passages on the two tracks (it is usually possible to do this by unplugging half of the input, or turning down the recording level). It is best to choose two passages from the same book, and for the passages not to include dialogue. Try to keep the loudness fairly even, and equal on the two recordings.

Ask subjects to listen to the passages through stereo headphones and to 'shadow' one of the passages – by repeating the passage as it is heard. Half of the subjects should shadow the left ear and half the right. Half of the subjects should have passage A to the left ear, and half passage B to the left ear (swap the headset round). Check for errors in shadowing. At the end of the period of shadowing, ask about the passage which is shadowed, and that at the unattended ear. You could also have some standard comprehension questions about each passage.

Is there a difference in recall or comprehension at the attended and unattended ear? What can subjects report about the ear which is not shadowed? Why do we need to have some subjects shadow one ear and some the other? Why do we switch the headset for half the subjects? Does it make a difference if the reader of the two passages is not the same person – or of the same sex? Do we get the same effect if we just instruct the subjects to attend without shadowing? Why do we get these effects?

Box 2.1

Subjective contours and apparent depth: a direct test

It has long been clear that the particular contours (outlines) present in the geometrical visual illusions are important in creating the illusory effect. A surprising, and quite recent, discovery is that **apparent** contours can also produce the illusion. These contours are not actually there – they only appear to be there.

A particular demonstration of this effect was reported by Coren and Porac in 1983. They studied the stimulus patterns which are shown in box figure 2.1.1.

The apparent contour can be seen in patterns A and B. It appears as if there is an upright triangle in the centre, just as in pattern C where the contour (the triangle) is actually present. The illusion which results in pattern A is that the white area which would be enclosed by the apparent contour, inside the triangle, appears brighter than the surrounding white paper although it is not. In pattern B, the central area appears blacker than the surround. The same effect is produced when the contour is actually present (as in C) although it is less marked. Another variation of the apparent contour

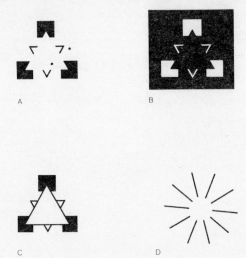

A   B

C   D

BOX FIGURE 2.1.1 · *The stimulus patterns used by Coren and Porac (1983)*

Based on material in S. Coren and C. Porac, *Perception and Psychophysics*, 33 (1983), 197–200.

effect is shown in pattern D. This time the apparent contour is a circle, and again the central disc appears brighter than the surrounding area.

Coren and Porac wished to test the hypothesis that this illusion may partly result from apparent depth created by the apparent contour. They proposed that in pattern A the central 'triangle' appears nearer than the background, and so brighter. They decided to measure the apparent depth of the two parts of the figure which are indicated by the position of the dots in pattern A (they are 1° of visual angle inside or outside the apparent contour). This can be done by an apparatus involving polarizing filters and a half-silvered mirror. The pattern was back-projected on to a screen which was viewed by only one eye (eliminating true binocular depth cues). At the same time a tiny red bulb can be seen by both eyes. This bulb is mounted to the right of the subject on a sliding track so that the subject can move it left or right. However, the image of the bulb is reflected in the half-silvered mirror, placed at 45° in front of the back-projection screen so it appears superimposed on the pattern. As the subject actually moves the bulb left and right, it appears as a red spot moving nearer and further in front of the subject. The subject simply moves the red spot until it appears to be as far away as the part of the pattern over which it lies. In this way, the exact apparent depth of any part of the pattern can be measured.

Twenty subjects with normal vision and naïve about the illusion were tested on all four patterns and with two spot placements in each. The patterns were presented in random order and the order of spot placement was also random. The subject made two settings for each trial, one moving the spot in from far away, and the other moving it out from very near, in counterbalanced order. The whole procedure was repeated twice for each subject, giving four readings for each pattern and spot-placement combination. These four values were averaged.

This experiment therefore has each subject performing under all experimental conditions. The independent variables are the pattern (four conditions), and the spot-placements (inside or outside the contour – apparent or real). The dependent variable is the apparant depth setting (averaged from the four values). The effects of order of testing are randomized. The effects of the starting-point (near or far) in setting the spot are balanced.

The mean apparent depth values, for inside the contour (Figure) and outside the contour (Background) for the four patterns, are shown in box table 2.1.1. Analysis of variance showed there to be a significant difference over the whole experiment between the settings for inside and outside the contour ($F = 19.28$, df = 1,19, $p < 0.001$). Separate t-test analyses for each pattern showed that this was true for each pattern (all four pairings, $p < 0.01$). In each case the spot was set closer to the subject when superimposed inside the contour rather than when superimposed outside.

BOX TABLE 2.1.1 *Settings of apparent distance (cm) from the observer for figure and background for the four stimulus configurations labelled as in box figure 2.1.1*

Target location	Stimulus configuration			
	A	*B*	*C*	*D*
Figure	31.1	30.9	35.1	31.9
Background	42.3	42.0	40.6	37.8

Further analysis of variance also showed that the apparent difference in depth was not equal across all patterns ($F = 4.412$, df $= 3,57$, $p < 0.01$). There was no difference between the size of the effect in pattern A and in B (mean depth effect 11.2 cm), but this effect was significantly greater than with either pattern C or pattern D (mean depth effect 5.7 cm).

The experiment shows that apparent contours, besides creating the illusion, can also generate apparent depth. The difference in apparent depth which is created is very marked (26% of the depth of the background). The apparent depth created is also significantly greater than that created when the contour is actually present. Whatever the explanation for the effect of apparent contours in generating the illusion, it appears that apparent depth has some part to play. The experiment also provides one illustration of how a purely mental cognitive phenomenon which has no physical basis can have a measurable effect upon sensory parameters (the brightness and depth).

Box 2.2

Individual differences in magnitude estimation of loudness

It is known that there are large individual differences in estimates of subjective loudness. When people judge loudness, their judgements do not exactly correspond to the physical stimulus. For example, to produce a given apparent change in loudness only needs a small physical change with quiet sounds, but needs a much larger physical change with loud sounds. The relationship between subjective and physical loudness seems to follow Stevens' power law. This can be stated as

(power law formula $\psi = k\phi^n$)

and simply means that the subjective value, ψ, is equal to the physical value, ϕ, raised to a power (by the exponent n) and multiplied by a constant k (to give the correct units). However, all you need to realize is that it is the exponent (n) part of the equation which varies between subjects and which can be used to describe the way in which loudness is being judged on any given occasion. The exponent is an index of the particular scaling which a given individual is using.

The aim of the present study was to see whether these individaul differences are stable: that is, whether, although different people may make different judgements, they tend to make the same judgement on different occasions. The subjects were 18 males and 4 females between the ages of 15 and 31. Each subject made magnitude estimates twice, with a gap of 11 weeks between the two occasions. In each testing session, which lasted about ten minutes, subjects heard 26 1 kHz tones lasting 0.5 sec and generated by a computer. The tones were presented binaurally through headphones and the subjects sat in a sound-attenuated (quiet) chamber. The tones varied in loudness from 30 to 90 dB SPL (Sound Pressure Level) in steps of 5 dBm, with each of the 13 stimuli being presented twice. After each tone, the subject typed a number to indicate its loudness, and then pressed another key to initiate the onset of the next tone. The presentation was therefore self-paced. Subjects were told to use any numbers they felt appropriate, but to make the ratios of their numbers proportional to the ratios of the loudnesses.

Subjects were randomly assigned to two groups. One heard the same random sequence of tones on both testing occasions. The other group heard a different random sequence. This was done to control for possible sequence effects. The

Based on material in A. W. Logue, *Perception and Psychophysics*, 19 (1976), 279–80.

BOX TABLE 2.2.1   *Summary of exponents and correlations*

		Stimulus order for two sessions		
Session		Same	Different	Total
First	Mean	0.26	0.25	0.25
Second	Mean	0.28	0.25	0.27
Total	Mean	0.27	0.25	0.26
Correlation		0.69**	0.58*	0.59***

* $p < 0.10$ ** $p < 0.05$ *** $p < 0.01$

second testing session was at the same time of day as the subject's first session. Thus tones employed are controlled by being fixed (the same on both occasions), and the time of day and instructions to the subject are similarly controlled.

The exponent n was calculated for each subject for the two occasions of testing. (The exponents were calculated for each subject at each session by using a geometric mean of subjects' responses at each decibel level and fitting a line to the averaged points by the method of least squares.) A correlation could then be calculated between the values of n for each subject, on the two testing sessions.

The mean values for the exponents on the first and second occasions, and their correlation are shown in box table 2.2.1. This table also shows the results for subjects receiving the same or different orders on the two occasions. The results are clear. There is a significant correlation between the exponents obtained from particular subjects over a period of 11 weeks. The correlation is rather higher for the group receiving the same rather than a different order, but the difference is not itself statistically significant. Over the whole experiment, the correlation between exponents is highly significant ($r = 0.59$, $p < 0.01$).

Despite the 11-week interval, subjects did show consistency in loudness estimation. This may be due to individual physiological characteristics, or it may be due to a learned pattern of responding in making loudness judgements. The relevant contribution of these factors has yet to be determined. However, it can be concluded that there are stable and lasting individual differences in the scales which subjects use in making magnitude estimates of loudness. This is a well-designed experiment, with controls for all the main factors which seem relevant including, for example, the time of day at which testing took place. The number of stimuli presented might be thought to be small, but stable estimates of the subjects' performance are obtained and so little would be gained by extending the experiment. In so far as Steven's power law is a good description of the relationship between subjective and physical properties (and there is little doubt that it is) then the experiment can be expected to have yielded reliable and valid results. If the experiment has any limitations, these are not in methodological design but rather in the interpretation of the findings. It is certainly interesting that individual consistency in judgements can be shown to operate over such a lengthy period. It would be much more interesting to know how this consistency is achieved, but the current experiment can throw little light on the processes which underlie these subjective judgements.

3

The Cerebral Cortex

The Structure of the Cortex

You will recall from chapter 1 that the **cerebral cortex**, the outer layer which covers the whole brain, is where intelligent function is carried out. It is here that thinking, language, memory and much of perception are performed and where complex acts are organized and initiated. At least part of the rich variety of conscious experience we enjoy as humans comes from the activity of the cortex.

The human cortex is, in contrast to the brains of other animals, covered by a mass of ridges and furrows (figure 3.1). These ridges and furrows are thought to be a biological adaptation which has allowed a greater surface area of cortex to be fitted inside the skull without expanding the head to an unacceptable size. One of these ridges is known as a **gyrus** (pl. gyri) and one of the furrows as a **sulcus** (pl. sulci). If you inspect a series of human brains, it is hard to spot the regularity in these **convolutions**. However, the pattern is less variable than first appears and most of the principal gyri and sulci have been named.

There are two main sulci which you should be able to spot fairly easily. One is the main fissure which runs back across the brain (see figure 3.2) and which is known as the **lateral** or **Sylvian fissure** or **sulcus**. The second is not always so easy to find, but runs more or less straight down from the crown of the head. This is the **central** or **Rolandic fissure** or **sulcus**.

These landmarks are combined with others to divide the surface of the brain on each side into four **lobes**. These are known as the **frontal**, **temporal**, **parietal** and **occipital** lobes. The division is a little arbitrary but is universally accepted. In neuropsychological analysis further subdivisions of the lobes are sometimes made, but often functions cannot be more accurately assigned than to one of the four lobes. The general orientational terms (see figures 3.1 and 3.2) may be used to indicate a more precise location within a lobe, as in the 'anterior parietal lobe' or 'inferior posterior frontal lobe' for example.

The most obvious feature of the cortex of the brain is that it is divided into

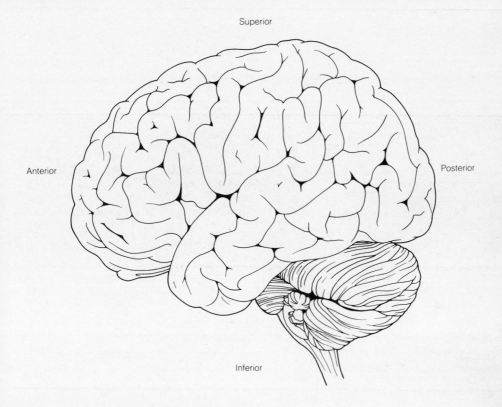

FIGURE 3.1   *Lateral view of the brain*

two lateral halves: a left and a right **hemisphere**. The cortex of the two hemispheres is anatomically similar, although there are some important differences. We will see that there are also important functional differences between the two sides of the brain. A section across the brain (figure 3.3) shows that the cortex of each hemisphere is quite independent of the other. The two are connected by the principal **commissure**, the **corpus callosum**, and by some smaller commissures but not directly in any other way.

What produces the appearance of the 'grey matter' of the cortex is the presence of a huge number, about 10^{10}, of the cell bodies of neurons. These neurons connect to structures in every level lower down in the brain and spinal cord and also form myriad connections among themselves.

Although we often consider the brain as an information-processing system, and the network of neurons as functioning like some kind of electronic machine or computer, it is a very difficult task to sort out just what any particular part of the system contributes to the operation of the whole. The interconnections among parts are very complex and each part

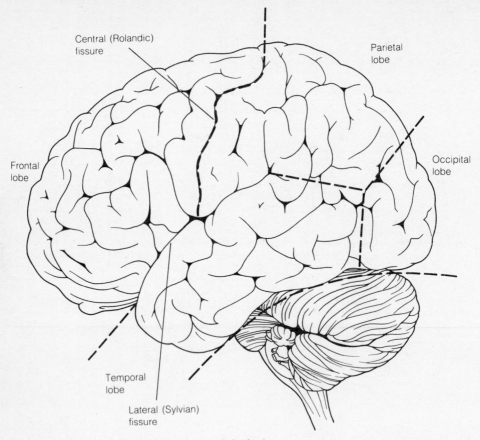

Central (Rolandic) fissure

Parietal lobe

Frontal lobe

Occipital lobe

Temporal lobe

Lateral (Sylvian) fissure

FIGURE 3.2 *Lateral diagrammatic view of the brain*

may carry out a variety of functions. As a result, there is no precise map of where particular functions are performed in the cortex.

You would find disagreement among neuropsychologists about whether the relative lack of precision in assigning functions to the cortex is because the system is complex and there is yet a lot of basic research to be done before we can describe it accurately, or whether we are partly at fault in thinking of the brain as if it were an electronic machine.

In what follows in this chapter it will also be useful to keep in mind a rough division of the cortex into three different levels: **primary**, **secondary** and **tertiary** cortex (see figure 3.4). Primary cortex serves the basic sensory and motor functions, while secondary cortex turns sensations into perceptions. The tertiary cortex serves the 'higher' intelligent functions. This division is partly, but not accurately, linked to the types of neuron found in each of the three levels.

Primary cortex is that part of the cortex where functions can be most accurately located. The cortex here does seem to be relatively specialized in

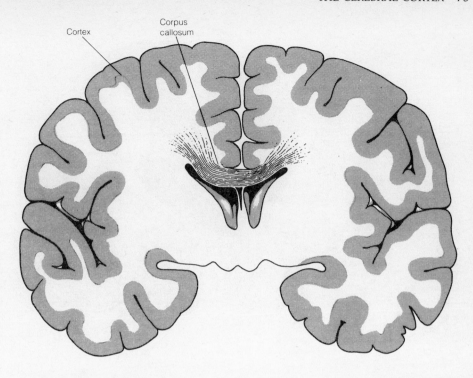

FIGURE 3.3   *A cross-section of the brain showing the cortex and the corpus callosum*

terms of quite small groups of cells carrying out specific jobs. It receives sensation from the special senses of vision and hearing as well as from touch. This has been shown in the classic stimulation studies carried out by Penfield from the 1950s onwards (Penfield, 1975). During an operation where the brain has been exposed, and the patient allowed to return to consciousness, the brain may be electrically stimulated (this is painless as there are no sensory receptors in the brain matter itself). Patients stimulated in primary sensory areas report basic sensory events. In visual cortex they may report flashes of white light with a particular location but no colour or form. In auditory cortex they may report a pure tone, or in somatosensory cortex a touch on a particular part of the body which they cannot otherwise describe. Stimulating primary motor cortex will produce a simple movement of a particular part of the body.

Secondary cortex is adjacent to the primary cortex. Its function seems to be to convert sensations into perceptions. Stimulating secondary cortex in vision may produce a report from the patient that it is as if some object can be seen. Its form and colour may be described – perhaps it looks like a woman in a green hat – and its name given. In addition the patient may seem to hear a tune playing or the sound of a person's voice. In touch the patient may say that it is like being rubbed on the leg with sandpaper, or

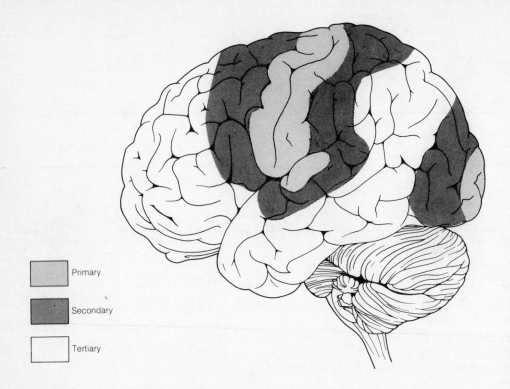

Primary

Secondary

Tertiary

FIGURE 3.4   *Diagram of three levels outlined on the cortex*

being brushed with velvet. Secondary cortex seems to interpret the sensation so that the experience becomes meaningful.

Tertiary cortex, also referred to as **association cortex**, accounts for almost all of the remaining cortex. It is in this cortex that higher level integration among the sensory modalities and with motor functions is carried out. It is the area where planning and thinking are performed and where memories are laid down and recalled. It is where learning and problem solving take place. It is the least precisely organized, and the least well understood, of the regions of the cortex.

There is one exception to this general pattern of the three levels of cortex, organized in a more or less symmetrical way across the two hemispheres. This is the subsystem which serves speech and language. We will consider this subsystem in detail in the next section. It comprises a number of specialized centres, and is also highly lateralized: that is, it is present in only one of the two hemispheres. For almost all right handed individuals, and more than half of left handers, it is located in the cortex of the left hemisphere.

Speech and Language

Structures in the language subsystem

There are four main elements in the structures which make up the language subsystem, normally located in the left cerebral hemisphere (see figure 3.5).

The first element is in the posterior superior region of the temporal lobe, in an area known as **Heschl's gyrus**. This area is involved in auditory perception and must be the starting-point for the reception and comprehension of spoken language.

The second element is a group of structures which make up the posterior language centres. They are not far from Heschl's gyrus and include **Wernicke's area** also in the superior, middle and posterior parts of the temporal lobe; an area around the posterior end of the Sylvian fissure known as the **peri-Sylvian association cortex**; and further towards the back of the brain, two regions known as the **angular gyrus** and the **supra-**

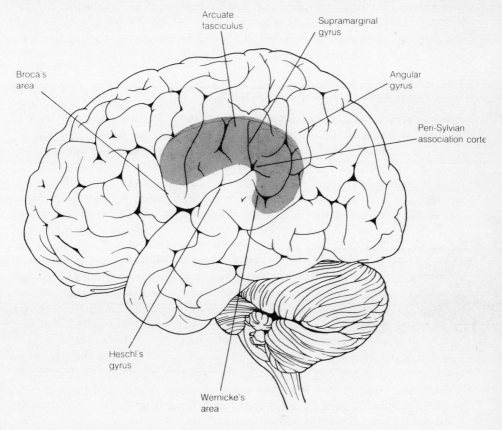

FIGURE 3.5   *Lateral diagram of the brain with language structures*

marginal gyrus. These areas are all quite close together and have important connections among themselves.

The third element is the anterior language centre, **Broca's area**. Broca's area is in the inferior posterior frontal cortex, just in front of where the central fissure comes down to a little above the Sylvian fissure. Both Broca and Wernicke were scientists who, in the second half of the last century, discovered the regions which bear their names.

The final element in the system is the **arcuate fasciculus**. This structure is, as its name indicates,. a curved bundle of fibres which forms a major connecting pathway between two areas of cortex. The two areas which it connects, passing back down into the brain between them, roughly correspond to the anterior and posterior language centres.

This description gives the impression that these elements can be very precisely located. This is unfortunately not strictly accurate. If the actual positions of lesions producing the classic signs associated with, say, Broca's area are carefully plotted on a map of the brain, it is found that they are scattered quite widely. Some do not even include the region known as Broca's area. However, the best sense that can be made of all the observations is by assuming the existence of the above elements and assigning them to the positions given. You should, however, recognize that the situation is not as neat and tidy as it might appear (cf. figure 3.5).

Functional elements of the language subsystem

Another way to analyse the language subsystem is in functional, rather than anatomical terms. This can be done by studying the forms of language difficulty (**aphasia**) which follow damage to the brain and looking for common elements in the problems which patients experience.

An enormous variety of classifications of aphasia have resulted from this approach, but the most widely accepted and most useful for psychologists is the Boston classification. In its simplest form this scheme suggests five different forms of aphasia (Kertesz, 1979).

Broca's aphasia has *speech output* as the main difficulty. It is a nonfluent form of aphasia. Patients with this form may understand more or less normally what is said to them or what they read. However, their speech has become restricted so that in severe cases they may even be mute. In the patients who retain some speech, the spoken output is sometimes referred to as 'telegraphic'. The content of speech becomes limited just to the key words and verbs, as it might be in a telegram. The order of the words is normal, and it is often possible to make some sense of what the patient is battling, with enormous effort, to say, but the adjectives, adverbs and subtleties of expression all tend to disappear. Short catch-phrases or automatic phrases may well be used, often inappropriately. Patients may also produce **phonemic paraphasias**, getting the sounds of parts of the words they are trying to say wrong, although it is often possible to guess the word which was intended. Difficulties in repeating exactly speech which is heard, or in naming things, may well follow from the main difficulty of speech output. The problem presumably lies in some general language output system.

Wernicke's aphasia is, by contrast, principally a disorder of language *comprehension*. Patients with this form of aphasia produce a normal quantity of speech, but have relatively severe difficulties in understanding what is said to them, or what they read. This, however, also seems in many cases to affect the content of the patients' speech. In some patients it may be normal, but in others may be quite unintelligible. This is because it becomes filled with both **semantic paraphasias** and with **jargon**. A semantic paraphasia is where the patient produces a word which does not have the intended meaning, although it may be related to the intended word ('red' for 'green' or 'table' for 'chair', perhaps). Jargon is the production of nonsense words. Whole utterances may be filled with jargon as in the case of a patient describing what a pen is used for: 'This is a tape of brouse to make buke deproed in the auria.' The structure of the sentence is English-like, but the meaning is quite indecipherable. Naming is often affected, as is repetition of words or sentences. In addition, written output may be as disordered as speech. It may be that the problems in speech output result from the difficulty in language comprehension. If the patients cannot understand language, perhaps they are for the same reason unable to monitor the language they themselves are producing. The result is the characteristic 'word salad' of Wernicke's aphasics, resulting from failure of some general language comprehension system.

The third form of aphasia is **conduction** (or central) **aphasia**. Here the patient can understand speech and read more or less normally. Spoken speech may be relatively normal, although there may be some limited difficulty of a kind similar to that of the Broca's aphasics. The principal difficulty seen in this form is a severe impairment of repetition. The patient understands what is heard or read, and may well be able to give an account of it in her or his own words, but will be unable accurately to repeat it exactly in its original form. A similar problem may be seen in reading aloud even though the patient seems to understand the meaning perfectly well when the material is read silently. Presumably, if Broca's aphasia and Wernicke's aphasia can be linked, respectively, to disorders of a language production system and a language comprehension system, then conduction aphasia results from the interruption of the direct link between them. The meaning can be passed from the input to the output system, but not in its exact literal form. Hence the name 'conduction' for this form of aphasia.

Anomic aphasia is the fourth form, and is probably the most common. Anomic aphasics understand speech and read normally, and they produce more or less normal speech in terms of both its quantity and content. However, they suffer from a specific difficulty in finding correct nouns and in naming objects. This can have an effect on their speech by producing hesitations while nouns are being sought. Sometimes a slightly inaccurate noun will be substituted as the patient cannot find just the right word, or things may be expressed in a clumsy way as the patient tries to get around the difficulty. The patient is rarely helped by prompting, by being given the initial letter, or a rhyming word. However, amazingly, the patient may spontaneously use the word which cannot be found, when it occurs as a verb. The patient shown a comb, might say, 'No . . . it's what you comb your hair with, but I don't know what it's called.' There is obviously a part of the system which, given a particular meaning, retrieves the appropriate word-form from some store. It is this which is disordered in anomic aphasia.

The **transcortical aphasias** are the final form. Here the problem is to some extent in both the comprehension and production of both speech and writing. A distinction is sometimes made between forms in which the greater problem is either **sensory** or **motor**, but both aspects tend to be affected in all the patients. What makes these patients unusual is that they do not understand what they hear, are more or less unable to produce normal speech, but can nevertheless repeat, parrot-like, what is said to them. Their repetition of the speech which they hear is more or less normal. This is almost the exact opposite of conduction aphasia. In transcortical aphasia we assume, therefore, that the direct route between the input and output systems is intact, but that there are faults affecting other aspects of both the input and output systems.

These five forms of aphasia are summarized in table 3.1. Of course it is often the case that particular patients do not fall clearly into a single category. Some patients are also so grossly disordered as to be described as **global aphasics**.

These five forms of aphasia relate remarkably well to what has already been said about the anatomical structures serving language (figure 3.5). If we examine the location of lesions which give rise to each of the five forms, we find that Broca's aphasia is associated with the anterior speech areas. Wernicke's aphasia is produced by lesions at the posterior end of the temporal lobe. Conduction aphasia can be linked to damage to the arcuate fasciculus, and anomic aphasia to the angular gyrus. This leads us to a tentative model of the language subsystem. Auditory input arrives in the region of Heschl's gyrus, and is then passed to the adjacent Wernicke's area

TABLE 3.1   *A classification of aphasic difficulties*

Aphasia	Fluency	Speech and writing	Repetition	Naming	Comprehension
Broca's	X	errors	limited	limited	√
Wernicke's	√	errors	limited	limited	X
Conduction	limited	√	X	limited	√
Anomic	√	√	√	X	√
Transcortical	X	X	√	X	X

√ = reasonably normal
X = definitely impaired

where speech comprehension is carried out. The stores which hold the representations of words (or the systems that access the stores) are associated with the nearby angular gyrus. The arcuate fasciculus then provides a direct route of transmission (although there must be others) forward to the anterior language areas, especially Broca's area, where language output is organized. The transcortical aphasias are associated with other anterior speech areas when the main difficulty is with speech output, or with the posterior peri-Sylvian association cortex when the difficulty is more in comprehension. This is undoubtedly a grossly oversimplified picture of the system and where it is located in the brain, but it does fit remarkably well the evidence which has so far been gathered.

Difficulties in reading (**alexia, dyslexia**) and writing (**agraphia**) tend to go along with difficulties in understanding speech or in speaking, but sometimes occur independently. There has been a great deal of research in the past few years into **acquired** dyslexia, a failure of reading in those who have once been normal readers, and how it may relate to **developmental** dyslexia, a failure to learn to read normally. When damage to the brain produces an acquired dyslexia, it is usually in the region of the angular gyrus and the supramarginal gyrus. Various subtypes of dyslexia have been identified, at least one of which is similar to developmental dyslexia. These studies have been very fruitful in assisting cognitive psychologists to refine their models of the normal reading process. A better understanding of how, in psychological terms, normal reading is performed has enabled neuro-psychologists to describe more accurately the difficulties which alexic patients are experiencing. This in turn should mean that more effective treatment strategies can be developed to help these patients overcome their problems (Kirk, 1983; Pirozzolo and Wittrock, 1981).

Recovery from aphasia depends, among other things, upon its cause and its severity. Aphasia resulting from a head-injury is likely to have a better outcome than when it results from a stroke, a loss of blood supply to part of the brain following the blockage of part of the arterial system. This may be partly a function of the fact that head-injury tends to occur in younger individuals than do strokes. The more severe the aphasia, the less recovery there is likely to be. Recovery from severe disorders may be very limited indeed. When recovery does occur it tends to be fastest in the first three months after the onset of the illness, with a slowing down after six months, and only limited improvements beyond a year after onset. There are few good studies of whether therapy of aphasia is effective, but some evidence that it can be successful. Most recently popular have been schemes to re-establish language by specific teaching programmes. Information about the patient's linguistic deficits is translated into a training schedule designed to improve the deficient aspects. This may be achieved either by practice of the area in which the problem occurs, or by teaching the patient strategies which enable the problem to be evaded. Good psychological and linguistic models of how language functions operate are essential if this approach is to be successful (Code and Muller, 1983).

Lateralization of language

We have already noted that the language subsystem is lateralized to the left cerebral hemisphere in the majorty of individuals. The evidence for this comes from a number of sources.

The first source is directly from patients who suffer unilateral brain damage: damage to just one hemisphere of the brain. The picture is complicated by the fact that some people have brains which are very strongly lateralized, while others have brains in which speech and language are to a more or less equal degree represented on both sides of the brain. Such people have a relatively bilateral representation of language. However, the frequency with which aphasia follows damage to either the right or left hemisphere alone can provide some information about how common different patterns of lateralization are in the population. A recent survey of all such studies between 1935 and 1975 by Satz (1979) suggested that for right handed patients, 95 per cent had language lateralized to the left hemisphere, in 5 per cent it was lateralized to the right, but that in no significant proportion of patients was it bilateral. The picture was different for left handed patients, with only about 75 per cent having language lateralized to the left hemisphere, none with speech in the right hemisphere, but 25 per cent with bilateral language representation.

Another source of information is the Wada Test. This is a procedure used to determine the side of language representation prior to certain forms of neurosurgery. Sodium amytal, which temporarily suppresses the activity of the brain, is injected first into one internal carotid artery, and then into the other. In each case, the activity of the hemisphere on the side of injection is disrupted for a period of about five minutes. It is possible to see whether suppressing the left hemisphere, the right hemisphere, or either hemisphere, interferes with the patient's speech and language functions. Typical results from Rasmussen and Milner show that, excluding patients who may have suffered brain damage early in life, of 140 right handers, 96 per cent had left sided language, 4 per cent right sided language, but none had bilaterally represented speech and language. Of 122 left and mixed handers, in 70 per cent language was in the left hemisphere, in 15 per cent in the right hemisphere, and in 15 per cent represented bilaterally. These figures show a good general agreement with the findings from studies of aphasia.

A further, though less important, source of information comes from psychiatric patients who have been treated with electroconvulsive therapy (ECT) for depression. It has become more common in recent years for unilateral treatments to be administered, with the two electrodes providing the shock being placed on the same side of the head. This reduces some of the side-effects which may include a temporary disturbance of memory and language functions. It is possible to study the severity of these language-related side-effects and to record how often they occur following either left or right sided treatment. The inference is that a left sided shock will disturb the left hemisphere more than the right, and particularly affect language functions if they are located in the left hemisphere. The results of these studies generally support the findings reported above (Warrington and Pratt, 1981).

We can also study the relatively rare cases in which one hemisphere of the brain has been removed (**hemispherectomy**), or in which the two hemispheres have been separated by division of the corpus callosum (cerebral **commissurotomy**). When a hemisphere is removed in childhood, either because of disease or to relieve a spastic motor handicap, the child generally develops relatively normal speech, irrespective of which hemisphere is taken away. However, removal of the left hemisphere in adults produces a severe global aphasia which does not usually follow right hemispherectomy.

Cerebral commissurotomy, or the split-brain operation, has been performed to improve certain severe forms of epilepsy. The corpus callosum is cut so that there are no direct links between the cortex of the left, and the cortex of the right, hemisphere (see figure 3.6 and also figure 3.3). It is possible to project language stimuli into just one of the two hemispheres. If a word or picture is shown briefly just to the left of where the subject's gaze is fixated (in the left visual field) it will be transmitted by the visual system only to the right hemisphere. If briefly shown on the right, it will go to the left hemisphere. The same logic will apply to letters, shapes, or objects felt by one of the two hands. If felt by the left hand, the information goes to the right hemisphere and if by the right hand to the left hemisphere. Once the information has arrived at one of the hemispheres, it cannot be passed across to the other hemisphere because the corpus callosum has been cut.

Studies of split-brain patients provide evidence for clear lateralization of *speech* to the left hemisphere. The patients can speak about letters, words, sentences, or objects which are projected to the left hemisphere through the right visual field or by the right hand. They cannot speak about information projected to the right hemisphere, and about which the left hemisphere is ignorant. However, this does not also apply to other language functions. It appears that although the left hemisphere is better at performing almost all language functions, the right hemisphere has nevertheless significant abilities, speech apart. The right hemisphere seems to be able to understand quite complex linguistic material, but is simply unable to respond by means of speech.

The work with split-brain patients has led to laboratory methods being developed which can be used with normal healthy subjects. These are discussed later in the chapter (pp. 95–7), but briefly, visual or auditory stimuli are projected into either the left or right hemisphere alone. Even though the corpus callosum allows information subsequently to be shared between the hemispheres, differences in response to the stimuli, measured in terms of either accuracy or speed, can be shown to depend on the hemisphere of original presentation. The results again support the evidence obtained from other sources (Gazzaniga and LeDoux, 1978).

The general conclusion is that in right handed subjects, language abilities

Normal subject:

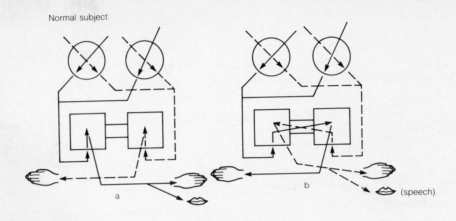

After commisurotomy:

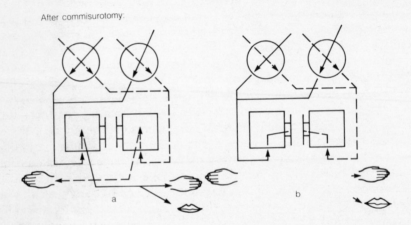

FIGURE 3.6 *Connections between the two hemispheres in normal and split-brain subjects, direct (a) and indirect (b) pathways. With the direct pathway, the right hand responds to the right visual field (solid line), and only one hemisphere, the left, is involved. With the indirect pathway, the left hand responds to the right visual field (solid line), and both hemispheres and the corpus callosum are involved. The direct pathway still operates but the indirect pathway is unable to function (After Beaumont, 1983)*

are relatively lateralized to the left hemisphere, with the strongest lateralization being for speech functions. Only a very small minority of right handed subjects have brains which are not organized according to this pattern. For left handers, this pattern is still typical of the majority, although the lateralization may not be so strong. A significant proportion of left and mixed handers seem to have brains in which speech and language functions are represented in both the left and right hemispheres.

The Control of Movement

The control of movement is not only one of the major functions of the cortex, but also illustrates how diverse areas of the brain co-operate in even apparently quite simple tasks. The basic control of movement can be considered in terms of two subsystems: the pyramidal and extrapyramidal motor systems.

The pyramidal motor system

The pyramidal motor system provides a direct pathway from the pyramidal cells of the primary motor cortex, the strip just in front of the central fissure, down to the midbrain and on to the spinal cord where links are made with the peripheral nervous system. Control then flows out to the muscles. At the level of the brain stem about 80 per cent of the fibres cross over to the opposite side so that control is predominantly **contralateral**, one hemisphere controlling the opposite side of the body. There are some contributions to the system from other cortical areas, from the secondary premotor area in the frontal lobe, from the sensory strip just posterior to the central fissure, and from other regions of the parietal lobe. The main feature of the system is nevertheless a direct route from the cerebral cortex out to the muscles.

The motor strip is organized in a highly topographic fashion. That is, it is possible to map the relationship between areas of the cortex and the parts of the body whose movements they control quite precisely. Stimulation of one of the cortical areas will produce a quite distinct movement of the appropriate body part. The map of the motor strip which has been derived from stimulation studies (figure 3.7) shows that the toes are at the top and

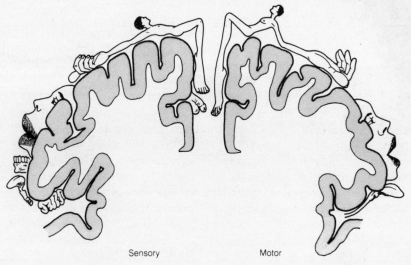

FIGURE 3.7   *Topographic organization of the sensory and motor cortex (After Beaumont, 1983)*

the head at the bottom of the strip. Each area of the body is associated with an area of cortex which is not proportional to the physical size of the body part, but to the complexity of movement which is possible with that part. So the legs or trunk, with only gross movements, have a relatively small amount of cortex controlling them; the hands and face, with a rich variety of fine and highly controlled movements, have a large area of cortex to control them. Damage to the pyramidal system generally produces not total loss of movement but rather weakness and imprecision (**paresis**).

The extrapyramidal motor system

The extrapyramidal system is more complex, simply because it encompasses all those elements of the motor control system outside the pyramidal system. It is made up of structures in the thalamus, the cerebellum, the basal ganglia (see chapter 1 and figure 1.3), and non-pyramidal elements in the motor cortex. The thalamus passes information to the cortex and to the cerebellum and receives input from both the basal ganglia and cerebellum. The cortex in turn passes messages to the basal ganglia and the cerebellum. The cerebellum probably has a general supervisory role organizing the smooth co-ordinated action of groups of muscles, and maintaining balance and posture. The thalamus is the central controlling element, but only under the supervision of the movements planned and organized through the cortex and basal ganglia.

This system is organized in a much more diffuse fashion than the pyramidal system. Damage to the system tends to produce both abnormal and disordered movements. Injury to the cerebellum may result in tremor and poor co-ordination when movements are carried out. Balance may be lost and walking becomes unsteady and clumsy. Injury to the basal ganglia may, by contrast, result in a resting tremor. You may well have seen elderly people suffering from Parkinson's disease, in which the limbs show a continual steady tremor which disappears when an intended movement is carried out. The old person may, to your surprise, pour the cup of tea quite competently, but distract them while they are holding the cup and the tea will very likely be spilled (Pincus and Tucker, 1978).

It is difficult to say just where voluntary movement is initiated in the brain. The cells in the motor cortex fire before some motor movement, but cells in other parts of the extrapyramidal system become active before that, so perhaps the motor cortex only acts when it receives information from other parts of the brain. The cerebellum seems to be involved in the activity both before and after the cortical cells fire. The control of movement, once the decision to initiate it has been taken, moves down a progressive hierarchy of command with increasing precision of control at each stage. In this way, a general intention can be progressively transformed into a sequence of highly specific commands to individual muscles. This is the principle involved in hierarchical command theory.

The role of frontal cortex

The primary level of motor control occurs in the motor strip, with the secondary level in the surrounding premotor cortex. The tertiary level of motor control is provided by the regions more anterior to this, known as the prefrontal cortex. Here complex motor acts are planned and programmed, and sequences of acts adapted to particular circumstances. These are linked with other functions of this area of the brain: problem solving and concept formation. Patients with damage to this region find difficulty in co-ordinating a series of actions which must be organized in a temporal sequence. For example, the patient may be able to mimic a single facial gesture quite competently, but unable to mimic a simple sequence of three such gestures. The difficulty might be seen in planning a series of movements to solve a paper-and-pencil maze problem.

The use of language to regulate complex skilled actions may be relevant here. Nearby areas of the frontal lobe deal with speech output and word production. We know that verbal mediation – the use of explicit self-instruction – may assist children to perform acts they would otherwise find too difficult. For instance, at a certain age, a child might find it impossible to press a button when a green light is illuminated, but not to press when a red light comes on (a go/no-go task). Teach the child to say out loud 'Green – press', or 'Red – don't press' before responding, and the task can be performed. Perhaps as adults we may use the same kind of mediation, but do it internally. You may be aware of 'talking to yourself' as an aid in the learning stage of some complex activity. Perhaps such assistance from language, but at an unconscious level, is used in much skilled motor activity, and is carried out within the frontal lobe. Whatever the reason, patients with damaged frontal lobes have difficulty in the high-level organization of motor performance (Luria, 1973).

The role of parietal cortex

The parietal lobes also make a contribution to motor control. Certain **apraxias**, which involve the loss of intentional movements, result from damage to the parietal region. It is important to remember that the more anterior parts of the parietal lobe contain the primary and secondary somatosensory cortex, providing perception of bodily stimulation, movement and position. Understanding and interpreting the external spatial world, and relating the spatial arrangement of the body to it, are all carried out in associated parietal regions. It is not surprising, given that motor activity can hardly be organized without reference to the position of the body and the position of objects in the external world, that the parietal lobe also makes a contribution to the control of movement.

Apraxias may affect almost any form of intentional movement, although gross movements of the body and limbs are more commonly affected. The patient may, strangely, carry out the relevant movements automatically, but be quite unable to initiate them by conscious intention. A drink might be taken quite automatically and successfully from a cup during the natural course of a meal. Ask the patient to demonstrate how to drink from a cup, with the cup present or not, and she or he may not be able to do so. Damage to the right hemisphere normally affects actions with the left hand. Damage to the left hemisphere principally affects the right hand although it may have an effect on both hands. This might again be because language systems (in the left hemisphere) contribute to motor control.

There are two special forms of apraxia. One is dressing apraxia. This is a disorder which specifically affects dressing movements. Patients with dressing apraxia end up, often after considerable effort, with their clothes on in the wrong order, with garments on back-to-front and inside-out, and legs in sleeves, and so on. No one seems to know why dressing should be such a specific ability, but it does point to what a specialized and complex activity getting dressed actually is (Weinstein and Friedland, 1977).

There is also constructional apraxia. This results in a failure to be able to produce properly organized drawings, or to fit the elements of a two- or three-dimensional problem together in the correct relationships. This is typically demonstrated with tasks involving building up simple arrangements of blocks, or copying patterns made up with little sticks. The central problem seems to be in understanding how the component elements relate to the correct final solution, and then in bringing them together and organizing them in the appropriate spatial relationships. It is more commonly found, and is more severe, following right sided parietal lesions (Benson and Barton, 1970; and see box 3.1).

The control of movement, even so simply described, shows how contributions come from many parts of the brain: from the frontal and parietal lobes of the cortex as well as from subcortical structures and the cerebellum. If you consider that in complex skilled acts vision and hearing will also play a part, as will memory and motivation, then it begins to seem as though the whole brain plays some part. To some extent that is true. Parts of the brain do have relatively specialized functions, and that is what neuropsychologists focus their attention upon, but you should also remember that in any real-life everyday situation, action involves the continual interplay of the whole constellation of cortical functions acting in an integrated and well-co-ordinated fashion.

Localization of Function

Relative localization

It will be clear from what has already been said that, with the exception of some specialized areas of primary cortex, particular psychological functions do not have a precise localization in the cortex.

From the 1860s, when Broca demonstrated the link between inferior posterior frontal left cortex (Broca's area) and speech production, there was an intensive search for the precise localization of function. By the turn of the century highly detailed maps were being produced, showing exactly which functions each small area of cortex carried out. These maps were based on **localizationist theory**, which enjoyed a moderate but qualified success.

Almost from the outset there were opponents to this view. Those who supported **equipotential theory** believed that precise mapping of functions was not possible. They pointed to observations that damage to different sites in the brain could produce the same handicaps. It was held that the effects of damage to the brain depend less on *where* the brain is damaged than on *how much* of the brain is damaged – the mass of the lesion. This theory has had a number of influential supporters.

The evidence about the location of the language subsystem within the brain, presented above, shows that there must be at least some degree of localization in the brain. However, the failure to demonstrate accurate and precise localization for the majority of functions, over a century after Broca's initial observations, shows that the strict localizationist view cannot be correct.

A third possibility is provided by **interactionist theory**, derived from the work of Hughlings Jackson around the turn of the century. His view was that 'higher level' functions are founded upon a number of more basic component skills. The component skills may be quite accurately localized, but are combined together to generate higher-level processes in flexible ways. The form of these combinations will depend on the task, on the individual, and may change over time. Because we only examine the patient's ability at the higher level, we are not able to see the localization of the basic components. We only see the varying pattern of localization which relates to the shifting combinations, appearing to us as a relative lack of localization.

The most popular contemporary view is partly derived from this position. Current cognitive psychological models which view the brain as an information-processing system fit very neatly with the interactionist theory. Component information-processing skills can be seen as basic modules in the system, their combinations being governed by task demands, cognitive strategies for task performance, and the flexible allocation of the resources available for processing. Psychologists interested in linking together cognitive models of normal function and neuropsychological models of abnormal function have had some success in recent years. Although such research is at a preliminary stage, it appears as if it may be possible to identify the sites of component processes by cognitive analysis of the performance of patients with lesions in particular cortical areas.

Sometimes linked to this position is a theory known as **regional equipotentiality**. This suggests that equipotentiality exists, but only within relatively well-defined regions of the cortex. This would certainly fit with the current state of knowledge which is generally able to assign a given function to some particular region – a lobe, or part of a lobe – but not to achieve more accurate localization within that region.

The position adopted by most neuropsychologists at the present time can be summarized as **relative localization**. It recognizes that most functions cannot be accurately localized, but assumes that if our analysis were more sophisticated, then it might be possible to demonstrate more precise localization. The increased sophistication might be in terms of anatomical determination of lesion sites. It would be helpful to specify more precisely the regions of the cortex affected and, perhaps more importantly, the linking pathways which have been interrupted. Alternatively, it might well be in terms of more sophisticated psychological analysis. If it were possible to describe in greater detail which elements of the cognitive performance system were not functioning correctly in a given patient, then the relationship between basic components and regions of the brain might become clearer. The most influential modern theories are clearly based on views of this kind, although some choose to emphasize the connections between processing modules rather than the processing modules themselves (Walsh, 1978).

Behind all these theories about brain localization lies the realization that we frankly do not understand how the brain operates. We may understand fairly well how individual groups of cells work, in terms of either an electrical or a chemical model. But when we consider vast numbers of neurons and the way in which they perform high-level complex functions, we really do not have any idea about how the results are achieved. Nevertheless, we have made progress in understanding the broad functional layout of the brain. The model of the brain as an information-processing system, operating in some ways like a computer, has been a helpful one. It has enabled quite productive theories to be developed which have not only made sense of the data, but have also been useful in guiding the treatment of brain-injured patients.

However seductive the 'brain as computer' model may seem, we should remember that it is just a model. In some ways the brain *is* like an electronic data-processing machine or computer, but in other ways it is not. The digital computer, for instance, operates rapidly and single-mindedly upon limited but high-quality data. The brain, by contrast, works slowly, but can tolerate extremely poor-quality and diverse data, and can operate flexibly and adaptively with its resources divided according to attentional demands. We should not lose sight of the fact that it is really a biological and not an electronic machine. There may well be some fundamental aspect of its mode of operation which we have not yet grasped. That is just one of the exciting challenges of contemporary neuropsychology.

Clinical evidence of localization

The logic which underlies clinical studies of localization is quite simple. It is only necessary to collect enough case material from patients who have suffered relatively well-defined damage to the brain, record the particular difficulties which they suffer, and then correlate the difficulties with the areas of the cortex which have been damaged. This is indeed what clinical neuropsychologists have been doing for the last century. The enterprise turns out to be not quite so simple when the logic is put into practice.

Part of the difficulty, of course, lies in accurately determining which parts of the brain have been affected. Careful selection of patients can help in this; also, recent developments in medical-imaging or making 'brain scans' have made this less of a problem. Descriptions of the patients' difficulties in functional terms are also inevitably rather crude, although recent developments in psychology are helping to improve their sophistication.

More of the difficulty lies in the fact that damage does not occur to the brain in a random fashion, and that in consequence it is difficult to control for all the other factors which affect the patient's performance while its relationship to the site of lesion is being studied. We know that among the factors which affect the outcome of brain damage are the following:

site	within the cerebral hemisphere
hemisphere	left or right
mass	extent of the lesion
cause	tumor, injury, stroke, disease
age	of the patient
acuteness	recent or long-standing lesion
stability	stable or developing lesion

If we want to establish that, say, the left frontal cortex is associated with verbal fluency, we first need an appropriate test. Asking the patient to generate as many words as possible beginning with a particular letter of the alphabet, in a given period of time, would do quite well. We then need a whole series of patients with clearly described lesions of different parts of the cortex. We hope to show that all the patients with left frontal damage are impaired on verbal fluency. We must also show that none of the patients without left frontal damage show an impairment in verbal fluency. But, we must be careful that the groups of patients either with, or without, left frontal damage do not differ on any of the above factors except for site. Otherwise, we shall not know whether to attribute any difference which we find in performance between the groups to the different sites, or to the differences on the other factors (Golden and Vicente, 1983).

In practice it is difficult to control for the factors not under investigation. Suppose that we choose to study only patients with a particular kind of tumour – perhaps tumours which grow and press on the brain but do not invade it. (We suspect that different types of tumour may produce different effects.) We will find that tumours of this type grow much more frequently over certain regions of the cortex than over others. When found in certain locations, a tumour may be very untypical of its type. It will be difficult to complete our survey of all the relevant sites over the cortex.

We might alternatively take missile wounds. Each major war around the world produces a great deal of neuropsychological case material. For the interests of science (although not those injured) modern gunshot wounds are excellent case material. They occur in otherwise healthy young men, the site of the lesion is accurately identified, and modern missiles most commonly pass directly through the head causing a surprisingly small amount of damage apart from producing a narrow track of disturbance as they pass. However, if we examine our case material we will find a preponderance of cases with frontal and occipital injuries. Soldiers injured by bullets entering the frontal or occipital lobes are more likely to survive as the missile may pass through without disturbing some of the central subcortical centres essential to life. Injuries with temporal or parietal entry points are more likely to lead to death or fundamental handicap. As a result, we shall again be frustrated in our efforts to build up a balanced and well-controlled research sample.

As a final example, perhaps we decide to simply compare left and right sided lesions from surgical cases. Surgical cases have the advantage that the surgeon can accurately describe the location and mass of the lesion introduced during the operation. However, it is commonly found that right sided surgical lesions are larger than left sided ones. This is partly due to the fact that patients are more likely to become aware of a developing problem at an early stage if the tumour or disease is developing on the left. This is because it is more likely to interfere with speech and language functions which are more readily noticed by the patient or his family and friends. As a result, medical referral will be earlier, surgery will be performed sooner, and the surgical removal may be smaller. In addition, surgeons may feel a little more free to remove matter from the right side of the brain, as they are less anxious about undesirable effects on language functions. We shall end up finding that our groups differ not only in hemisphere of lesion, but also in mass of lesion, and we shall be unable to disentangle the effects of the two factors.

It is necessary to give examples of these problems in order to explain why neurospsychology has not made more progress than it has. Despite these difficulties of undertaking sound research, it has been possible to build up quite an extensive picture of where psychological functions are located within the brain. In rather crude and general terms, it is possible to summarize the findings to date by table 3.2.

There was, for many years, a debate about the location of intelligence within the brain. In particular, it was thought by some that intelligence was generated by the frontal lobes. This seemed to be confirmed by the studies of Halstead and others in the 1940s. Halstead proposed the idea of 'biological intelligence' which supposed that intelligence was based upon adopting an 'abstract attitude': that is, that actions are governed not so much by external objects around us as by what we *think* of them. It involves the abilities of concept formation and categorization. He measured biological intelligence by a comprehensive battery of tests and concluded that greater deficits were found with frontal lobe damage.

This work was followed up by Teuber and colleagues studying patients injured during the Second World War, but they failed to find any evidence

TABLE 3.2 *Some specific functions associated with the cortical lobes*

Frontal
  motor and premotor
      primary and secondary motor control
      verbal fluency
  prefrontal (anterior)
      tertiary motor control
      response adaptability
      planning sequences
      verbal regulation
      problem solving
      eye movements
      memory for recency
  Broca's area
      expressive speech
  orbital cortex (inferior)
      personality
      social behaviour

Temporal
  anterior
      personal experience
      sexual behaviour
  superior
      auditory sensation and perception
      reception and comprehension of speech and writing
      musical abilities
  middle and inferior
      tertiary visual function
      perception of faces
      auditory–visual integration
      long-term memory
      paired-associate learning

Parietal
  anterior
      sensation and perception from the body
      body sense
      visual object recognition
  posterior
      intentional movement
      constructional ability and drawing
      reception of spoken language and reading
      spatial orientation and attention
      route-following and right–left discrimination
      calculation
      tactile–visual integration

Occipital
  anterior
      visual perception
      reading
  posterior
      primary visual sensation

that general intelligence is exclusively linked with the frontal lobes. At the same time, re-analysis of Halstead's data showed that the frontal lobe-damaged patients which he had studied had larger lesions than those patients with damage in other areas of the brain, casting doubt on his original findings. Modern work has continued, on balance, to fail to find a link between intelligence and the frontal lobes (Teuber, 1964).

It now seems much more sensible to think of intelligence as being made up of a whole set of interacting abilities. These abilities may be located in various regions of the brain. It makes sense to think of the whole brain as being intelligent, but not to assign intelligence to any one particular part. That the frontal lobes seems to be more 'intelligent' than the rest of the brain probably just reflects the fact that the frontal lobes account for over half the tertiary cortex of the brain. It is therefore possible to suffer larger lesions of the frontal lobe, and for frontal lesions to affect more of the separate abilities that go to make up intelligent behaviour. Modern psychological theories of intelligence have also recognized its complexity.

The importance of localizing functions in clinical patients goes beyond scientific curiosity. It is also important for the diagnosis and treatment of disorders in individual patients. Until recently, the main focus of clinical neuropsychological practice was diagnosis. Psychology had an important part to play in the localization of lesions in particular patients. Particularly when the only other information came from neurological examination, from recordings of the electrical activity of the brain, and from certain specialized and slightly risk-laden X-ray techniques, then the clinical psychologist's assessment of the patient's difficulties and the likely site of the associated lesion could be of critical importance.

The clinical neuropsychologist still makes an important contribution to the clinical team, but the advent of safer physical-imaging techniques with better resolution – the forms of 'brain scan' now produced by computerized axial tomography (CAT), by nuclear magnetic resonance (NMR) and by positron emission tomography (PET) which enable images to be created of 'slices' through the head – has made a significant impact on diagnostic accuracy in locating lesions (Wiederholt, 1982).

The emphasis has therefore now shifted to an analysis of the patient's difficulties in psychological terms. Accurately specifying what the patient can and cannot do within a psychological model can form the basis for decisions about the management and treatment of the patient's condition, and about rehabilitation. Training programmes can be accurately targeted to improve the patient's performance in areas of handicap. Adjustments can be made to the patient's environment and life-habits based upon the existence of continuing disability. We can expect this to be a growing area of concern for clinical neuropsychology.

Lateralization of Function

In studying brain-damaged patients in order to find out how the normal brain works, we assume that the damaged area has stopped working correctly, but that the rest of the brain carries on more or less as normal. This may, or may not, be a reasonable assumption. In terms of localized functions we have no choice but to make what sense we can of the clinical case material: that is, the brain-damaged patients we happen to come across. However, with regard to lateralization, it is possible to study the operation of the normal healthy brain as it performs high-level psychological functions by using one of several recently developed techniques.

Lateralization refers to differences between the two cerebral hemispheres: to the idea that certain functions are carried out more effectively or more efficiently by one of the two hemispheres. There is then said to be a functional asymmetry, or a 'hemisphere advantage'.

It has been clear for a long time that damage to a particular part of the brain in one hemisphere may not have the same effect as damage in the same location in the other hemisphere. Some of the clearest evidence comes from language functions. These were discussed earlier in the chapter (pp. 82–4) and we have also noted hemisphere asymmetries in motor functions. Another clear example is associated with the anterior temporal lobe. Damage to this area on the left produces a difficulty in the long-term recall (say, after an hour) of a short story, but not of a complex abstract drawing. Damage to the same area on the right has the opposite effects. The left hemisphere is therefore associated with long-term verbal memory, while the right is associated with long-term nonverbal memory. Many such asymmetries have been reported in brain-damaged patients. The split-brain patients have also provided evidence of hemisphere asymmetries in the lateralization not only of speech and language, but also of other functions.

The techniques

The laboratory techniques which can be used with normal subjects have been developed from those used with split-brain patients. They rely upon the presentation of lateralized stimuli which enter only one of the two hemispheres. Most of the research has been carried out in the visual and auditory modalities.

In vision, the procedure is known as the **divided visual field** technique. In a typical experiment, the stimuli to which the subject must respond are presented in a tachistoscope (a tachistoscope allows exposure of a visual stimulus for a brief, controlled duration). The subject is instructed to fixate upon some central point. The stimulus, usually a word or a simple form or line drawing, appears for less than 200 milliseconds to either the right or the left, about 2 to 6 degrees of visual angle from the point of fixation. The duration of the stimulus is too short for an eye movement to be made to the stimulus position, and the subject cannot anticipate its appearance as it occurs randomly to the left or right. The stimulus will therefore be projected in either the left or right visual field, and because of the anatomy of the visual pathways (see figures 2.3 and 3.6) it will be transmitted into the contralateral hemisphere, and into that hemisphere alone. The subject's task will typically be to name the stimulus, pick it out from an array of possible stimuli, or match it to another stimulus. How rapidly the subject responds, and whether the response is correct, will be recorded. The experiment described in box 3.2 uses this technique. Although the brain is free to share the information between the hemispheres after its initial reception, it has been found that with various stimuli and various tasks, a lateral asymmetry can be observed. The subject will do better when the stimulus is initially presented to one hemisphere rather than the other (Beaumont, 1982).

In audition, the most common technique is **dichotic listening**. Unfortunately, the projection of the auditory pathways up to the cortex is not purely contralateral (see figures 3.8 and chapter 2). Information presented to one ear can go to both hemispheres: to the opposite hemisphere by the contralateral route, and to the hemisphere on the same side by the ipsilateral route. If different stimuli are presented to the two ears simultaneously, then there will be competition between the stimuli to travel up to the cortex by the ipsilateral and contralateral pathways. However, there is good reason to believe that in this case the stimulus at a particular ear goes to the opposite hemisphere. At the cortex, the information arriving by the contralateral pathway is dominant over that arriving by the ipsilateral pathway. This is the basis of the dichotic listening technique. Words, sentences, music, or environmental sounds are carefully synchronized and presented simultaneously to the two ears. The accuracy of report or speed of response to a stimulus is recorded, and lateral asymmetries in terms of the superiority of one of the ear–hemisphere combinations can again be found (Springer, 1979).

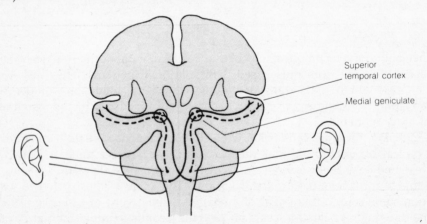

FIGURE 3.8   *The auditory pathways. The pathways which cross (solid line) are larger than the uncrossed pathways (dotted line) and are dominant.*

These are the techniques which have been used most commonly in the research, although there are others. These include the use of tactual stimuli; recording the lateral deviation of gaze; differences in performance with the left and right sides of the body; and direct measurement of electrical activity, blood flow and metabolic changes in each hemisphere of the brain.

The findings

As there is reasonable agreement among the findings obtained with the various techniques, they can be considered together.

The left hemisphere is generally found to be at an advantage in tasks which require identification of 'verbal' stimuli, whether these are words, letters, meaningless strings of letters, or numbers. The same will be true if the stimuli are to be matched rather than identified (see box 3.2 for a study of this kind). The fact that the stimulus must be analysed for its abstract symbolic meaning seems to be important. Simply analysing the perceptual characteristics such as the shape of the stimulus does not produce a left hemisphere advantage. However, the advantage does not seem to get stronger as the linguistic complexity of the stimuli increases. Abstract nouns do not produce a stronger left hemisphere advantage than concrete nouns; nor do words for which it is hard to generate an image. Nonsense words – strings of letters which do not spell a real word – can also produce the left hemisphere advantage, whether or not they are pronounceable (like 'BOV' rather than 'ZKP'). The advantage does not therefore lie simply in the involvement of linguistic processes. However, with dichotic listening, the fact that the stimuli are speech-like, if not actually speech, makes it more likely that a clear and stable right ear (left hemisphere) advantage will be found.

The advantages found for the right hemisphere are generally less strong than those found for the left hemisphere. However, they generally involve tasks or stimuli which are 'nonverbal' in character. Randomly generated irregular shapes produce a right hemisphere advantage, as will any drawing or form which is difficult to name. Faces, whether they are photographs or schematic composites, show a particularly strong advantage unless there are names very strongly associated with the faces. Certain more elementary perceptual characteristics will also produce the right hemisphere advantage, including brightness and colour, depth, motion and stimulus enumeration. Complex musical stimuli will produce a left ear (right hemisphere) advantage in most subjects, as will environmental sounds (taps running, or cars passing) or 'nonverbal vocal tract sounds' (coughs, belches and hiccoughs). Pitch perception may, or may not, provide a right hemisphere advantage; in the context of speech-like material it may be associated with the left hemisphere, while in the context of musical stimuli, it may be associated with the right (Young, 1983).

The models

How can we explain these lateral asymmetries? There are two types of model which have been proposed: structural and attentional.

Structural models suppose that the asymmetry appears because basic cognitive functions are localized in particular areas of the brain and are represented more strongly in one hemisphere rather than the other. If the task under study is better dealt with by the functions located in, say, the left hemisphere, then projecting stimuli into the left hemisphere will produce an advantage. This could be because the stimuli arrive by a more direct route at the hemisphere where they will be processed (if stimuli arriving at the 'inappropriate' hemisphere are subsequently transferred across the corpus callosum to the 'appropriate' hemisphere, this would be a more indirect route). Alternatively, the stimuli may arrive at a place where they will be more efficiently dealt with (in constrast to stimuli not subsequently transferred across the callosum).

Early theorists thought that the nature of the stimulus ('verbal' or 'nonverbal'), or the nature of the response demanded, might be what determines the asymmetry. More recent work emphasizes the importance of the cognitive processing required for the subject to carry out the task. Different tasks will involve different operations, and these will each be relatively if not completely lateralized to one of the two hemispheres.

Attentional models, by contrast, propose that each hemisphere can be more or less activated by particular task conditions. The expectation that a particular sort of stimulus will be presented, or a particular task be required, may 'prime' one of the hemispheres. It will be activated in readiness for that stimulus or task. Similarly, concurrent processing loads will affect the state of each of the hemispheres. If one hemisphere is busily engaged with one type of task, it may (if spare capacity remains) be active and ready to take on another task. On the other hand it may fall to the less occupied hemisphere to take up responsibility for the new task as it comes along.

In support of this latter explanation, it has been found that expectations about what stimulus or task will come next can influence the degree and direction of asymmetry observed. In addition, the results of a divided visual field experiment may be changed by requiring the subject to concurrently remember a list of words (engaging the left hemisphere) instead of remembering a short melody (engaging the right hemisphere). These are demonstrations of attentional effects upon lateral asymmetries.

Current opinion accepts that both structural and attentional factors are involved in producing lateral asymmetries. The structural factors are probably the more important. The two models are sometimes combined into a dynamic-structural model, but this does no more than suggest that structural lateralization exists, and that it can be modified by attentional conditions (Cohen, 1982).

It is, finally, important to remember that cortical lateralization of psychological functions is set in a context of general biological asymmetries.

Definite anatomical asymmetries between the hemispheres have now been established. Humans show a preferred handedness, and make greater use of one eye, ear and foot. There are asymmetries of the internal organs, the shape of the face, the hair on the head and palm-prints. There is almost no part of the body without its particular pattern of asymmetry. Such asymmetries occur throughout the natural and physical worlds. There is obviously an adaptive advantage in having a divided cortex, with various functions allocated differently to its two halves. The significance of this type of arrangement has only recently been recognized and its implications are now being very actively explored.

Physiological and Psychological Models

In this chapter we have ignored a serious and fundamental issue. This is a philosophical problem known as the 'mind–body problem'. It has dogged psychology throughout its history and is still unresolved. It is of particular relevance to neuropsychology.

As neuropsychologists we are interested in mental events (perceptions, thoughts, memories, beliefs, ideas, plans). We try to relate these to physiological events occuring in the brain – 'body' events. The problem is to know whether the mental events are really the same as the body events, but described and analysed in different terms; or whether mental events have a separate identity from body events. **Monist** views are held by those who believe that mind and body are simply different aspects of the same phenomena. **Dualist** views are held by those who believe that mind and body are separate and have independent properties. There is still a vigorous debate between these two schools of thought (Bunge, 1980).

The issue is important for neuropsychologists because, if the monists are correct, then it is perfectly sensible to look for the representation of mental events in physical states of the brain. Given the right techniques we should be able to identify feelings and thoughts in the electrical activity of the brain, or its biochemistry (although it may not be the most sensible or efficient way to identify them). If the dualists are right, however, we may be making a fundamental error in trying to relate mental and physiological events. The task may be inherently impossible.

Most neuroscientists seem to adopt a monist position, but one which still permits some special properties for psychological events (a position sometimes referred to as emergent psychoneural monism). Take the taste of sweetness, for example. We bite an apple and taste the chemicals which provide the experience of sweetness. We can expect to identify the brain mechanisms operating in the sensation and perception which is a response to those chemicals. The property of sweetness is, however, not in the chemicals but in our *experience* of tasting them. The sweetness is not in the apple (which is not sweet unless tasted), but in our mind when we taste the chemicals. Purely psychological events may emerge out of physiological events. This view is attractive because it means that psychology cannot be reduced to biochemistry, yet it allows for there being some essential relationship between what goes on in the mind and what goes on in the brain.

This is an exciting area because after centuries during which the mind–body problem has been open to analysis only by philosophers, it now looks as though it may be possible to investigate the problem empirically. New techniques of analysing the electrical activity of the brain (see chapter 4) may give us sufficient precision to observe, at one and the same time, specific cognitive operations and specific physiological events in the brain. Some technical problems remain, but we could be on the brink of an enormously significant leap forward in our understanding of how mental events arise out of physiological processes.

In the meantime, neuropsychologists continue to employ the sort of methods described in this chapter. Particular use is made of cognitive models of human abilities, usually formulated in terms of information-processing systems. At the same time, the anatomical organization of the cortex and its physiological systems are analysed and related, by clinical and experimental studies, to particular functional components of behaviour. These are described in terms of the psychological cognitive models. The result is a growing appreciation of how the cortex is organized and how it is able to generate intelligent behaviour.

Further reading

A broad introductory and non-technical text, which covers both clinical and experimental aspects of neuropsychology, is J. G. Beaumont (1983), *Introduction to Neuropsychology*, Oxford: Blackwell Scientific. Another broad and well-illustrated text, which considers normal and abnormal functions, is B. Kolb and I. Q. Whishaw (1985), *Fundamentals of Human Neuropsychology*, San Francisco: W. H. Freeman.

A clearly written introductory text on hemispheric differences is S. P. Springer and G. Deutsch (1985), *Left Brain, Right Brain*, San Francisco: W. H. Freeman. It concentrates on the experimental, rather than the clinical, aspects of neuro-psychology. A very thorough introduction to the theory and practice of clinical neuropsychology can be found in K. W. Walsh (1978), *Neuropsychology: A Clinical Approach*, Edinburgh: Churchill-Livingstone.

Discussion points

1 Neuropsychology has had only limited success in assigning functions to specific areas of the cerebral cortex. Why is this?

2 What do you suppose might be the biological and psychological advantages of having two, relatively independent, cortical hemispheres?

3 Discuss how an accurate functional description of a patient's disabilities after brain damage could be used to plan a programme of rehabilitation.

4 Take an everyday situation of performing some task and analyse the principal functions involved. Then relate these to the areas of the cortex involved by using table 3.2. You could choose playing a stroke at tennis or throwing a dart; replacing a motor-bike part; solving a crossword clue; sewing on a button; or speaking on the telephone.

5 Should we regard mental and physiological events as the same basic phenomenon, or not?

Practical exercises

1 On an unlabelled diagram of the brain, or on a model of the brain if you have one available, identify each of the cortical landmarks and locations mentioned in this chapter.

2 Obtain a pair of compasses with reasonably sharp points, but not so sharp that they might puncture the skin. They should be able to close almost completely. Select three or four sites on the body: perhaps the fingertip, the lower arm, the cheek and the lower leg. Establish the sensitivity of each of these body areas to light touch by measuring the two-point threshold. With the subject unable to see, perform a series of trials in which sometimes one and sometimes both points of the compasses (decided randomly) are lightly touched on the skin. Start with the compasses fairly wide and gradually decrease the distance between the points until the subject cannot tell whether one or two points have been applied. The two-point threshold is the largest distance between the points at which the subject cannot discriminate between a single and a double touch. Relate your findings to the sensory homunculus in figure 3.7.

3 Obtain some photographs of faces in straight frontal view. By cutting or by masking, observe how asymmetrical the faces are. If you can arrange to reverse the faces (by turning round a slide, or having them printed backwards), have judges (who are preferably not familiar with the faces) rate which version of the face is more expressive: the normal or the reversed orientation. If possible, you might arrange for composite faces to be made up out of two left or two right halves (one half normal, the other reversed) of an original face. Alternatively you could use a small mirror on edge down the centre of the face to produce the composites. Which of these is rated more expressive: the double-left or double-right face? If the people depicted are known to you, which is a better likeness of the person? Can you account for any differences you find in terms of lateral brain organization? Assuming you normally gaze at the centre of the face, is there a difference between the half-face you see in the left visual field, and the half-face you see in the right visual field? Is there a difference in the expression which the person produces on the left or the right side of their face?
   (See R. Campbell (1978), Asymmetries in interpreting and expressing a posed facial expression, Cortex, 14, 327–42; and J. K. Thompson (1985), Right brain, left brain; left face, right face, Cortex, 21, 281–97.)

Box 3.1

Constructional apraxia as a function of lesion locus and size in patients with focal brain damage

The aim of the study was to examine constructional apraxia as a function of lesion site and size. The subjects all had localized war-related shrapnel injuries documented by neurosurgical investigation.

On the basis of the hemisphere of the lesion and whether it was anterior or posterior to the Rolandic fissure, a total of 52 subjects were assigned to left anterior (LA, 17), right anterior (RA, 12), left posterior (LP, 10) and right posterior (RP, 13) groups. There were no significant differences between the groups in mean age, mean educational level, mean time since injury, or mean size of lesion. The groups were therefore matched on these factors. All the subjects were given the Wechsler Adult Intelligence Scale (WAIS), which includes a Block Designs subtest, requiring the subject to reproduce a printed design using coloured blocks; and the Bender Gestalt Reproduction Test in which subjects copy, by drawing, a series of simple abstract designs. All were able to understand the tasks, and none had any other relevant physical, sensory, or cognitive disorder. The independent variable is therefore the locus of the lesion (classified into four groups); the dependent variables are the scores on the two tests administered; and other factors are controlled by matching the groups or by assuming that they act randomly across the groups.

The researchers had some particular hypotheses in mind when they carried out the study. These were that (1) right hemisphere (RH) lesion patients would do worse than left hemisphere (LH) patients because the right hemisphere is thought to be involved in spatial and constructional abilities; (2) posterior lesion patients would do worse than anterior lesion patients because previous research has shown the parietal lobes to be involved in spatial and constructional abilities; (3) in the RH group, there would be higher correlations between the results of the tests because it is the factor common to the tests which is located in the right hemisphere. This last hypothesis follows from a belief that various factors influence test performance. These are not just the function which the test aims to assess, but also things like an ability to understand the instructions or to generate the responses. In this case, it is constructional ability which is common to the tests, and so a deficit in this ability will affect both tests equally, while other factors will vary in their effect upon the test results. The result will be a stronger positive correlation between the test results when constructional abilities, in the right hemisphere, are affected and are responsible for the deficits in performance.

Based on material in F. W. Black and B. A. Bernard, *Cortex*, 20 (1984), 111–20.

BOX TABLE 3.1.1   *Percentages of missile wound patients demonstrating constructional apraxia on selected variables*

	Block Designs (%)	Bender Gestalt (%)
Left anterior	29	6
Right anterior	8	25
Left posterior	20	20
Right posterior	46	46

It was found (using analysis of variance) that there were no significant differences among the four groups in WAIS scores (either in Full Scale IQ or Block Designs subtest). There was a significant effect of hemisphere (RH groups did worse than LH groups; $p < 0.01$) on the Bender Gestalt test, but no difference between anterior and posterior groups, and no interaction between the effects (i.e. the hemisphere difference was present between both RA and LA, and RP and LP groups).

The researchers went on to calculate the proportion of patients with abnormal scores for each group. Abnormal scores were taken to be scores at more than one standard deviation below the overall sample mean. The proportions of patients with abnormal scores are shown in box table 3.1.1.

Using a chi-squared analysis it was found that there was a higher incidence of constructional apraxia in the RP group, as shown by the Block Designs test, than in the other groups (chi-squared $= 4.67$, $p < 0.05$).

Correlations were also calculated among the results of the tests for each subject, using the Pearson product moment correlation coefficient. There were significant correlations ($p < 0.01$) between the Block Designs and the Bender Gestalt tests for the RA and RP groups, but not the LA and LP groups. These results only partially support the particular hypotheses which the researchers had. On the cruder measure of 'abnormal scores', the RP group did do worse on both tests, but neither hyothesis (1) nor (2) was entirely supported by the full analysis of the test scores. Hypothesis (3) was supported by the intertest correlations. The results therefore only provide weak support for the idea of a uniform syndrome of constructional apraxia which is represented more strongly in the right hemisphere and in its posterior portion.

The strengths of the study are its clear design and straightforward statistical analysis, with good control on variables not under examination. There are two main weaknesses of the study. The rather crude classification of lesion sites probably means that patients with 'pure' constructional apraxia are not being accurately identified. Also, the limited range of tests used and results presented means that further cognitive analysis of the deficits shown is impossible. None of the patients seems to have been particularly seriously impaired.

Box 3.2

Left and right lateralization for letter matching: strategy and sex differences

The aim of this study was to look for hemisphere asymmetries in two types of letter matching task. Subjects were asked to judge pairs of letters as being either *physical* matches (*AA* or *aa* but not *Aa* or *Ab*) or *name* matches (*AA*, *aa* and *Aa*, but not *AB* or *Ab*). The advantage of this is that it is possible to study two different cognitive tasks, using exactly the same stimuli: pairs of letters. This controls for stimulus effects.

The stimuli used were pairs from the letters *A,a,E,e,M,m,R,r*. They were presented for 100 msec in a tachistoscope (see p. 95). One letter was at the central fixation point and the other letter 2.73 degrees to either the left or right, in a random sequence. If the stimuli were the same one button was pressed, if different another button was pressed. The buttons were pressed with either the two index, or two middle fingers. Half the subjects used index fingers for 'same' and half for 'different'. There were 16 practice and then 96 experimental trials, half of which required 'same' and half 'different' responses. Subjects were told before each trial which principle of sorting (physical or name) to use, the two forms occurring in a random sequence. Reaction time was recorded. Trials which were responded to incorrectly, or which had responses longer than 1 sec, were replaced later in the sequence.

Thirty male and 30 female students completed the task. The independent variables were sex of subject, principle of sorting, and visual field of presentation; the dependent variable was reaction time. Order, practice and expectancy effects were controlled by randomization. Response factors were controlled by balancing the allocation of buttons, by using both hands, and by having half the trials associated with each response.

The mean difference in reaction time between scores for left visual field (right hemisphere) and right visual field (left hemisphere) stimuli was calculated. The mean results are shown in box figure 3.2.1.

There were no significant effects of sex of subject (from analysis of variance). The pattern for male and female subjects was the same, and they did not differ in level of performance.

A form of the *t*-test was used to examine whether the mean difference score under each matching condition differed from zero (no hemisphere difference). Under physical matching there was no significant difference from zero. Thus, although there was a tendency for a right hemisphere advantage in this condition (faster responses in

Based on material in S. J. Segalowitz and C. Stewart, *Neuropsychologia*, 17 (1979), 521–5. Copyright (1979), Pergamon Journals Ltd.

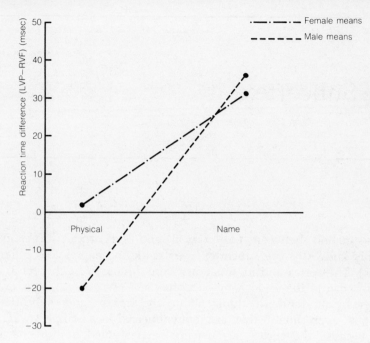

BOX FIGURE 3.2.1 *Mean difference in reaction time scores for left visual field and right visual field stimuli, for males and females, and for physical and name matching*

left visual field), there was no significant absolute hemisphere asymmetry for physical matching. For name matching, the mean difference was significantly different from zero ($p < 0.0001$) indicating a clear left hemisphere superiority (faster responses in right visual field) for name matching.

Other workers have found a significant right hemisphere advantage for physical matches. It would be interesting to know whether, in this study, mixing the two forms of matching trials into a single series has weakened that effect – perhaps by encouraging subjects to use a naming strategy, even on physical match trials. Would two separate blocks of trials for name/physical matches produce different results? It is a weakness of the study that this was not investigated. The strength of this study is its clear design and its control of stimulus parameters.

4

The Subcortex

The distinction between the cortical and subcortical forebrain (more generally known as the **subcortex**) was made in chapter 1 (see figures 1.2 and 1.3). The cortex and its functions were discussed in chapter 3, and we can now turn to the underlying subcortex.

Psychologists tend to think about the cortex and subcortex quite separately, even though they are interconnected in a complex way. This is partly because the cortex has usually been studied in humans and the subcortex in animals. As the cortex serves 'higher' functions including, for example, language it is difficult to conduct relevant studies with animals. As brain damage affecting the deeper areas of the subcortex often produces widespread behavioural disorganization, and the patient may well not survive, it is difficult to study subcortical function by observing brain-injured patients. Animal studies involving surgically placed lesions have more commonly been used.

However, damage to the cortex rarely avoids associated damage to underlying subcortical structures. The cortex is also in constant communication with the subcortex, influencing it and being influenced by it. Separate consideration of the cortex and subcortex is therefore to some extent artificial. Some attempts have been made recently to integrate these relatively separate areas of study (Dimond, 1980).

The functions of the subcortex will be considered under three main headings: emotion, arousal and awareness, and motivation.

Emotion

Physiological signs of emotion

The autonomic nervous system is the principal mechanism which governs emotional response. Its basic structure, in terms of the sympathetic and parasympathetic branches, was described in chapter 1 (see figure 1.6). Some of the effects of the ANS on various target organs were also illustrated (table 1.1). The links between the endocrine system and the ANS (see p. 22) were emphasized. These systems, working together, are able to produce a rapid and generalized response throughout the body to emotional situations.

The fact that the ANS has such widespread effects on target organs at the periphery of the body means that these effects are relatively easy to record. Psychologists are able to study physiological emotional responses *non-invasively* from the surface of the body. It is not surprising that these responses can be recorded at the surface of the body: it is presumably important for others to be able to perceive our emotional state in everyday social intercourse. Blushing is probably the most obvious example of this process. Typical measures of emotional response include heart rate, respiration rate, skin temperature, blood flow, blood pressure, muscle tension, and galvanic skin response (GSR).

GSR was one of the first emotional measures to be studied, and is still one of the most important. When an individual is emotionally aroused, the electrical properties of the skin change. This can be detected by measuring the electrical resistance of the skin, or by passing a weak and imperceptible current through the skin and measuring its conductance. Emotional events produce sudden and dramatic changes (the galvanic skin *response*), but there are also smaller shifts in the general level of resistance and conductance which are related to psychological arousal. These changes are related to sweat gland activity, although they cannot be entirely accounted for by the actual presence of sweat. GSR is usually measured from the palm of the hand.

All these measures can easily be taken by the use of **transducers** which detect the changes at the surface of the skin, and pass them to chart recorders or computers for storage and analysis. Study of these ANS measures is a specialized branch of physiological psychology known as **psychophysiology**. The principal recording device has been the **polygraph**, capable of recording a number of different measures simultaneously on different **channels** and displaying them on a chart (figure 4.1). The polygraph is rapidly being replaced by the laboratory microcomputer.

The polygraph is also popularly associated with the detection of deception as a 'lie-detector'. It has long been proposed by some that inspection of polygraphic psychophysiological recordings can determine whether a subject is telling the truth or not. The polygraph is widely used in the United States for security vetting, in criminal investigation and in employment selection. Scientific opinion is, however, clearly of the view that these procedures are insufficiently sensitive and reliable. Professional opinion in Britain is against their adoption (Lykken, 1983).

People do not generally regard their psychophysiological responses as under voluntary control. Heart rate, blood pressure and sweating are thought of as automatic physiological responses. We are often not even aware of changes in blood pressure, pupil dilation, or peripheral blood flow. However, it has become clear that with appropriate training, a certain

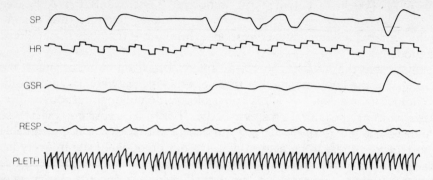

FIGURE 4.1   *A polygraph recording showing: SP, skin potential; HR, heart rate equivalent from each beat-to-beat interval; GSR, galvanic skin response; RESP, breathing; PLETH, plethysmograph of pulse amplitude taken from the finger. Recording taken during sleep and showing spontaneous changes in SP and GSR (From Venables and Christie,* Research in Psychophysiology, *copyright 1975. Reprinted by permission of John Wiley and Sons, Ltd.)*

amount of control can be gained over these responses. This often involves the use of **biofeedback** by which the activity of the relevant response is made visible or audible to the subject. GSR may be translated into a rising and falling tone which the subject hears, or heart rate may be shown as a varying level on a visual display. The subject is then able to learn how to exercise some control over the response system. This may be by cognitive mediation (thinking appropriate thoughts), by the use of certain muscle groups, or by more fundamental physiological control (Beatty, 1983).

At one time, it was thought that there would be significant opportunities to apply training in the control of autonomic responses to the treatment of a variety of disorders. Patients might be taught to reduce high blood pressure, or to control epilepsy. In the event, it turns out that the amount of control which can be achieved is rather limited. However, training techniques are usefully employed in controlling anxiety symptoms, treating excessive blushing, and to some extent in the control of heart rate and blood pressure. Some responses are easier to control than others. Heart rate is relatively easy, at least for some people (see box 4.1). Pupil dilation or piloerection (making the hair on your arm stand on end) is rather more difficult. You could try it: no complex equipment is needed to get feedback on changes in the last two responses.

Theories of emotional perception

How do our emotional feelings come about? Do they produce the bodily reactions of emotion, or do they follow these bodily reactions? The first theory about the relationship between feelings and the activity of the ANS was developed independently by two scientists at about the turn of the century. The theory is known by both their names as the **James-Lange theory**.

This theory proposes that emotional experience *follows* ANS changes at the periphery of the body. The sequence of events is that some stimulus is perceived by the brain and triggers off activity in the ANS. This results in changes in peripheral organs. These peripheral changes are in turn detected by the brain and result in the experience of emotion (see figure 4.2(a)). The James-Lange theory is therefore referred to as a **peripheral theory** of emotion. A typical sequence of events might be that a sudden noise from behind, perhaps a 'blood-curdling' howl, startles us. As a result our palms turn clammy, the heart starts to beat faster and blood pressure rises. These bodily changes are detected by the brain, and the experience of fear and alarm follows. Crudely put, the theory says that we are afraid because we run away, not that we run away because we are afraid.

Subsequently, in 1929, Cannon raised a number of objections to this theory. These included the observation that:

1 If the peripheral organs are surgically separated from the brain, this does not impair emotional behaviour. (Comment: this can be observed in humans with spinal injuries, although they have learned before injury to interpret various situations as emotional, and do even so report a certain lack of emotional feeling. It can also be seen

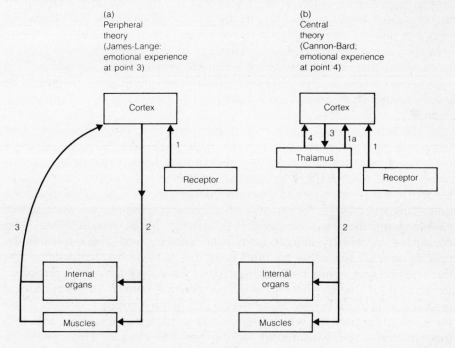

FIGURE 4.2 *The hypothesized sequence of events in autonomic emotional response for (left) a peripheral and (right) a central theory of emotion.*

in animal experiments, but these can only deal with emotional *behaviour*, not emotional *experience*.)

2 The same peripheral changes occur in different emotional states. If the changes do not differ, how can the subsequent emotions? (Comment: it is in fact still a matter of debate as to whether emotions can be reliably distinguished on the basis of the peripheral changes.)

3 The peripheral organs are too insensitive to allow for the range and quality of emotional experience. (Comment: in view of recent research, especially that involving biofeedback, some scientists consider that they are sufficiently sensitive. Our purely emotional experience is not, after all, so complex.)

Therefore, these objections are not so damning that the James-Lange theory must be entirely abandoned, but they do point to some real difficulties for the theory.

Cannon produced his own theory which was later extended by Bard, so that the theory is now known as the **Cannon-Bard theory**. This proposes that emotional experience is generated in the brain and does not depend upon peripheral changes. It is therefore a **central theory**. In this theory the sequence of events might be that the stimulus is perceived in the brain by the thalamus which in turn both passes information about the stimulus to the cortex and also triggers off responses in the ANS. There is then further intercommunication between the cortex and the thalamus in the control of the emotional response, and it is in this process of feedback from thalamus to cortex that the emotional experience arises (see figure 4.2(b)).

In the central theory, peripheral changes are not differentiated according to emotion, they simply represent a general **preparedness for action**. It is also not necessary for the pathways which detect peripheral changes to be intact, or that there should be a high level of sensitivity in the peripheral organs.

It is difficult to decide between peripheral and central theories of emotion because supporters of the two theories have undertaken different kinds of research. Supporters of a peripheral theory have tended to conduct studies of peripheral ANS changes in humans. Supporters of a central theory have tended to study animals and examine changes in the CNS. However, one important question is obviously whether it *is* possible to discriminate emotions on the basis of peripheral activity. Much research has been conducted in which subjects have been subjected to various emotional experiences, elicited either by films or by the behaviour of confederates of the experimenter, while psychophysiological measures have been recorded. In general, it seems that there is no general pattern of physiological response which can be said to be typical of a given emotional state, but that there might be patterns which are specific to particular emotions although these patterns will be different for different individuals. This concept is referred to as **response specificity** (Wenger, 1966).

A more recent development has been to recognize that what people think about a situation may influence their emotional reaction. This has produced **cognitive theories** of emotion which take account of how an individual perceives the situation and the associated ideas and expectations held about it.

An important demonstration of this type of theory is the **Schachter-Singer** experiment (Schachter and Singer, 1962). They had four groups of subjects. Three groups received injections of adrenaline, which should produce general sympathetic excitation. Of these groups, one was correctly informed about the expected effects of the injection, one was left ignorant about the effects, and one was misled about the likely effects. The fourth group simply received a placebo injection and was left ignorant as to its effects. The experiment deliberately varied the degree of physiological arousal (by administering adrenaline or an inactive placebo), and also the appropriateness of the explanation for any changes experienced. Subjects correctly informed could attribute the increased arousal they felt to the injection. Those misinformed could not attribute the arousal to the injection, and presumably had to find some other explanation for the increased arousal which they felt.

In addition, in this experiment, the cognitive aspects were manipulated by having confederates of the experimenter in the waiting room, who acted either angrily or euphorically in order to induce the same kind of feelings in the subject. Both objective physiological recordings, and subjective reports of emotional feelings, were subsequently taken.

The results are quite complex, but there are three important findings.

1 The group receiving the placebo showed and felt less emotional response than those injected with adrenaline. The adrenaline does, therefore, have a positive physiological effect.
2 Subjects correctly informed about the likely effects of the drug showed and felt less emotional response than those left ignorant or deliberately misinformed. They presumably attributed what they felt to the drug and so did not respond to the general situation as much as those who had the same feelings, but could not account for them by the injection.
3 The behaviour of the subjects, and their reports of how they felt, tended to follow the behaviour of the confederates in being angry or euphoric.

Therefore the experiment shows that the explanations which individuals have for their own feelings influence how they behave and feel. It also shows that the type of emotion can be influenced by the circumstances in which arousal occurs. Nevertheless, it shows that basic physiological changes in themselves can make people feel more emotional.

None of the three theories of emotional response – peripheral, central and cognitive – is entirely incompatible with the others. It is likely that all three types of process play some part in determining the rich variety of emotions which we feel.

Aggression

One aspect of emotion, aggression, has received particular attention from researchers. It is clear that the physiological mechanisms which control aggression also control flight (running away), and these behaviours are together referred to as **agonistic** behaviours. A variety of different forms of aggression can be seen in animals. These include aggression involved in hunting for food; aggression used in defending territory or young; aggression between males in competition for females; aggression used in personal defence when 'cornered'. Each of these has some parallel in human behaviour.

The principal method of investigating the neural basis of aggression has been by **electrical stimulation** of the brain (**ESB**) in animals. It has been found that stimulation of the hypothalamus in particular can produce aggressive responses in a variety of experimental animals. Laboratory cats, who do not normally attack rats, can be induced to mount an attack during hypothalamic stimulation. The attack behaviour ceases as soon as the stimulation ends.

It appears that three different kinds of agonistic behaviour can be elicited from three different areas of the hypothalamus. The first kind, **affective attack**, involves sympathetic arousal. In the cat the fur stands on end, the cat hisses, snarls and breathes deeply, finally springing on the rat with a scream and tearing at it. This is very like the defensive reaction of a cornered animal. By contrast the second kind of agonistic behaviour is referred to as **stalking attack**. This is like the behaviour seen in hunting: the cat creeps towards its prey, nose low to the ground, and quietly and efficiently grasps and bites the rat. The third kind of behaviour involves **flight** where, under stimulation, the cat simply turns and runs.

These three different forms of agonistic behaviour resulting from ESB in the hypothamalus have been identified in a variety of species, and are found in comparable areas in each. It seems to be a general feature of brain organization in mammals (Flynn et al., 1970).

Although stimulation of parts of the hypothalamus can increase the probability of these agonistic behaviours occurring, it seems that stimulation of other parts of this region will not reduce the likelihood of attack or flight. Other structures in the subcortical limbic system (see p. 6), particularly in the **hippocampus**, **amygdala** and **caudate nucleus**, also contribute by exerting either an excitatory or inhibitory influence on the hypothalamic centres. Taming, therefore, as well as wild uncontrolled aggression can be produced by stimulation or surgical removal of parts of these other subcortical structures.

Perhaps the most dramatic demonstration of the subcortical control of aggression has been provided by Delgado. He inserted electrodes in the

appropriate regions of the brain of a fighting bull. Armed only with a cape
and a radio transmitter capable of delivering stimulation to the bull's brain
through the electrodes, he entered the ring and showed that it was possible
to halt the bull in mid-charge. As shown by film recordings, the rather
confused bull merely turned and walked away. (plate 4.1).

Human aggression is a more complex phenomenon as it is considerably
modified by social control. The influence of the cerebral cortex, in terms of
the application of learned constraints on aggressive behaviour, is powerful
in modifying the operation of subcortical centres. However, in certain
conditions of damage to the brain, increases in aggressive behaviour can be
seen. Although it is infrequent, outbursts of aggression can occur in patients
suffering from temporal lobe epilepsy. These patients have an abnormality
of the temporal lobes which produces a characteristic kind of epilepsy. The
abnormality can affect the hippocampus, which underlies the temporal lobe,
and so increases the likelihood of violent episodes. Tumours of the limbic
system, although they often produce more widespread behavioural disrup-
tion, may in rare cases have the result of producing rage, particularly if the
tumour affects either the hypothalamus or the amygdala (Heilman and Satz,
1983).

Psychosurgery

Attempts have been made to control disorders of human emotion by
operations on the brain, and this surgery is known as psychosurgery.
Interest in this possibility stems from the case of Phineas Gage. An
American railroad construction worker, he had an iron bar blown through
the front part of his head in an explosives accident in 1848. He survived, but
lost a large portion of both frontal lobes and as a result he underwent a

PLATE 4.1   *A wild bull charges Dr José Delgado, who is armed only with a cape and a radio*
transmitter (left photo). When he presses the transmitter, the bull abruptly stops his attack
(right photo). The radio transmitter sends a mild current to electrodes implanted in specific
areas of the bull's brain (Photograph by José Delgado)

personality change from being a sober, responsible and family-loving man to being impulsive, wilful, inconsiderate and obstinate. A similar change can be seen in patients who have suffered damage to their frontal lobes in road traffic accidents.

Observations of the effect of such accidental injuries led to the introduction in 1936 of an operation known as **prefrontal leucotomy**. By a variety of methods, the aim of the operation was to sever the links between the frontal lobe and subcortical centres of emotion. It was widely used over the following 30 years, at first for the treatment of schizophrenia, and subsequently more often for severe anxiety and depression. Major studies of how effective this operation was did not appear until the 1960s, when it was agreed that the operation was not very effective and carried an unacceptable risk of death or unwanted side-effects. As a result, the operation fell into disrepute (Clare, 1980). Prefrontal leucotomy is still occasionally performed in carefully selected patients, suffering from severe and distressing anxiety and tension, for whom other treatments have not been effective and in whom there is a significant risk of suicide.

Modern psychosurgical techniques differ from operations like prefrontal leucotomy both by being more precise and by requiring smaller surgical lesions. The lesions are generally created by heating or cooling small areas of brain tissue, or by allowing the controlled release of radioactivity. The lesions are generally placed in the limbic system or basal ganglia. Some of the operations are thought to be effective for chronic anxiety, and others for obsessional states. Occasionally, patients with severe depression or chronic pain are also operated on. However, great care is taken in assessing the suitability of patients for these operations.

A further form of psychosurgery has been even more controversial. This is surgery aimed at the amygdala or hypothamalus in order to reduce severe and uncontrolled aggressiveness. Part of the opposition to this operation comes from its earlier use with violent offenders in the USA as an alternative to imprisonment. This has resulted in very strict controls on such operations in North America. In the UK, a very small number of such operations are performed each year. The operation appears to be effective in reducing emotional excitability, and in improving the patient's social adaptation, without significantly affecting the ability to perceive, think, or reason.

There are considerable ethical problems in deciding whether psycho-surgery should be more widely employed or not. Some have argued that it is improper to operate on apparently healthy brain tissue to modify a behavioural disturbance. This is likely to be seen as particularly unaccept-able if the behavioural disturbance is regarded as antisocial rather than being the cause of distress to the patient. There are very real fears that psychosurgery could become simply a matter of social 'mind-control'.

However, there are patients who suffer considerable and prolonged distress as a result of emotional disorders who might be helped by such operations. *If* the operations do work in such cases, why not allow the techniques to be used more widely? The problem is in deciding, scientifically, how effective they are. It is believed to be unethical to perform a study using a randomly assigned control group to analyse the outcome of such an operation. It is also difficult to assess just how much change has occurred, and to decide whether it is in the desired direction. Often patients are not independently assessed by experts disinterested in the outcome of the surgery. There is also the concern that the operation may dull all responsiveness, producing a rather 'cabbage-like' state, instead of selectively correcting the abnormality which is the reason for the surgery. Finally, are patients competent to agree to an operation of this kind, and should their relatives be allowed to take such decisions for them? If not, who should decide? (Valenstein, 1980)

For these reasons, there is a great deal of caution in the application of psychosurgery. There is some reason to believe that the modern operations can be effective if patients are carefully selected. However, in view of the problems of deciding exactly who the operation might benefit, and the widespread ethical doubts, it is probably sensible that further developments in psychosurgery be treated with some caution.

Arousal and Awareness

Brain mechanisms of arousal

A person's level of arousal varies, not just between waking and sleep, but along a broad continuum from keen alertness through drowsiness to deep sleep. In abnormal conditions arousal may drop further into coma. Normal variation in the level of arousal is produced by two types of change: gradual slow shifts in the general level of arousal (**tonic** changes) and more marked short-term changes (**phasic** changes).

The **reticular formation**, which passes through the brain stem, is probably the most important structure in regulating the general arousal level of the brain. As the ascending reticular activating system (ARAS) acts to detect the arrival of external stimuli, and then produces immediate and widespread activation of the whole brain, it has the effect of ensuring that the system is in a sufficiently alert state to deal with biologically important stimuli. If the ARAS is artificially stimulated it will wake a sleeping animal, and increase the level of alertness in an awake animal. Severe damage to the ARAS will produce coma and, eventually, death. Similarly, the descending parts of the reticular system also ensure that lower centres are active to receive commands when higher-level brain activity increases.

Other structures also contribute to the tonic changes in arousal. Also in the brain stem, the **locus coeruleus** can produce more than the normal amount of sleep if damaged, or increased alertness if stimulated. In chapter 1 it was noted that the hypothalamus has centres which can produce sleep or wakefulness. These structures are also under some control from the cerebral cortex. As the cortex is also influenced by the ARAS it is possible to see what a complex set of interactions there is among these structures. They are partly determined by the amount of external stimulation, and partly by changes in the internal physiological environment.

Arousal also follows a daily cycle, according to a **circadian rhythm**. Most biological functions show a daily repeating cycle of changes, and even body weight varies by a small amount through the day. An easy way to monitor such changes is by putting a thermometer in one's mouth; oral temperature rises through the morning, tends to drop back a little during the afternoon, then rises through the evening and falls back rapidly at night.

It is interesting that this cycle of body temperature, varying over about 2° during the day, tends to correlate roughly with performance on psychological tasks. The higher the body temperature, the faster and more accurate is performance. Problem-solving and reaction time tasks are usually best performed in the early afternoon and performed least well between 2 and 4 a.m. There also seem to be individual differences between those known as 'morning' and 'evening' types (figure 4.3). Morning types have the peak in their temperature cycle about an hour earlier than evening types. Morning types are generally up early, bright and breezy, but early to bed, while evening types are still bleary-eyed at mid-morning, but enjoy the night-life into the early hours. Personality differences of this kind may have some basis in differences in physiological arousal (see box 4.2).

Psychological studies of performance at different times of the day are important for tasks such as watch keeping in radar installations, air traffic control and industrial plant monitoring. Such tasks involve prolonged **vigilance**, and a decline in alertness can have serious consequences. Particularly if the tasks are performed by personnel on shift-work, it is

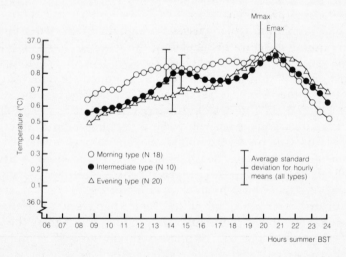

FIGURE 4.3   *Mean daytime oral temperature curves for morning and evening types (From Horne and Osterberg, 1977)*

important to know how the adaptation to different shifts affects arousal. It is clear that most workers take quite a period to adapt to a new shift working. Often, because shifts are rotated to minimize the working of unsocial hours, the worker may be changing shifts again just as soon as the adaptation has been achieved (Marks and Folkard, 1984).

These circadian rhythms are governed by internal biological clocks. It seems likely that these clocks are, at least partly, located in the hypothalamus. If they are kept in isolation from normal daylight cycles, individuals will maintain a regular cycle, although it will not be of exactly 24 hours, but usually a little longer. It seems that regular daily changes in the cycle of light and darkness serve to keep the clock regulated, but that they are not necessary to drive the clock.

Stimulant and **depressant** drugs will also regulate the tonic level of arousal. Many people drink coffee (and also tea) for the caffeine which acts as a stimulant and increases alertness. The opposite effects are produced by alcohol which is a depressant upon the CNS, and may be employed as a 'nightcap'. Other nightcaps such as milky drinks involve mild digestion and will be associated with parasympathetic activity of the ANS, which is de-arousing. Although people who smoke may say that it calms their nerves (and the ritual of smoking may do so), the physiological effect of nicotine is to arouse the CNS. You may see people in pubs unconsciously increase their rate of smoking to counteract the excessive and unwelcome depressant effects of the alcohol which they are drinking. In this way they can continue to be sociable while maintaining their level of arousal (although the nicotine does not counteract many of the other undesirable effects of the alcohol which contribute, for example, to unsafe driving).

People therefore act, through their diet and their daily habits, to regulate and control their physiological arousal. Nevertheless, this control is set against a regular daily pattern of variations in arousal, and a continually changing level of arousal in response to the degree of stimulation to which the individual is subjected.

Electrical activity of the brain

A direct way to observe physiological changes in brain arousal is by recording the electrical activity of the brain. This is most commonly done by using the electrophysiological technique of the **electroencephalogram (EEG)**.

The electrical activity of the brain can be quite easily detected by electrodes stuck on to the surface of the scalp. In some respects this is a crude measure because the electrode is detecting the activity over quite a large area of cortex which lies below it under the skull. It nevertheless gives quite a good guide to the general level of activity in the underlying region of the brain.

The potential difference (difference in voltage) between two electrodes is found electronically, amplified, and then written out as a continuous chart recording (figure 4.4). It is usual to record from a number of pairs of

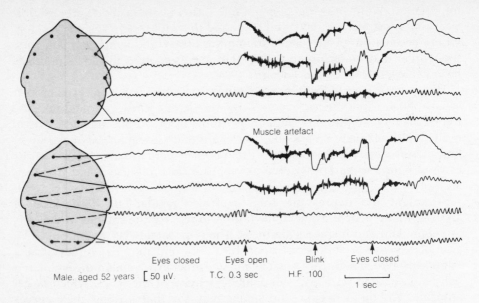

Muscle artefact

Eyes closed   Eyes open   Blink   Eyes closed

Male. aged 52 years   [50 µV.   T.C. 0.3 sec   H.F. 100   1 sec

FIGURE 4.4   *Normal Adult EEG recorded from four electrode pairs over the right of the head (upper) and left of the head (lower), and lasting about eight seconds. Note the alpha rhythm which is prominent over the rear parts of the head, and which disappears when the eyes open. When the eyes close, it returns. Note the artefacts caused by muscle movements of the eyes and face, and by blinks (From Pryse-Phillips, 1969)*

electrodes (channels) simultaneously. There are a set of standard electrode positions which are employed to investigate hospital patients, although these may be varied in research studies. The main way in which the complex waves are analysed is by their predominant frequency, and it is now usual for the EEG waves to be passed to a computer for analysis. However, the EEG is basically no more than the electrical difference between two brain regions, recorded at a number of different sites over the scalp (Binnie et al., 1982).

The EEG is of particular interest to psychologists because it reveals differences in arousal, including the arousal produced by performing mental tasks. One of the early discoveries about the EEG was that the pattern of activity altered as the patient went from relaxing with eyes closed to attending to the world with eyes open. This change can be seen in fig. 4.4. This change occurs not only upon eye opening, but also with active engagement in mental tasks – performing mental arithmetic, for example.

The change which occurs is one of **desynchronization**. The activity with eyes closed contains regular waves of large amplitude occurring at about 8 to 12 cycles/sec, known as the **alpha rhythm**. With mental engagement, this is replaced by less regular waves of smaller amplitude with a frequency between 12 and 30 cycles/sec, the **beta rhythm**. Because the alpha waves occur together across large regions of the brain, the alpha activity is said to be synchronized. The beta activity is much more variable from site to site, and so represents desynchronization. The amount of desynchronization reflects the degree of mental activity or arousal, and can be measured by calculating the relative amounts of alpha and beta activity in a given period of EEG recording.

Other frequencies can be seen in the EEG. **Theta** activity is between 4 and 8 cycles/sec. It is more common in children, and is also seen while adults are meditating. The slowest waves, **delta**, are abnormal in awake adults but appear during sleep. Particular types of waveform and other rhythms can be seen in patients suffering various disorders of the nervous system.

Most psychological research has concentrated on measuring the amount of alpha activity present, although there has been increasing interest in the type and amount of beta present. Modern computing techniques have allowed much more sophisticated analysis of EEG waveforms to be carried out. It is now possible to link the activity of certain regions of the brain with specific mental abilities. There are considerable technical difficulties in this research, but it is important and exciting because it allows us, for the first time, to observe with some precision physiological and mental events occurring together (Andreassi, 1980).

An alternative way of examining the brain's electrical activity is by recording **average evoked potentials** or **responses** (**AEPs** or **AERs**). This is another new technique made possible by laboratory computers. The idea is that if you present a simple stimulus to the brain, the normal EEG response that you see is made up of the brain's particular response to the stimulus embedded in a great deal of 'noise'. This 'noise' reflects all the other ongoing activity happening at the same time. If we can assume that this noise occurs randomly with respect to the timing of the stimulus (and it is a reasonable assumption), then we can collect a lot of samples of the brain response to a particular stimulus and add them together, so that the features which are present in each occasion will sum together and be preserved in the final waveform. The irrelevant 'noise' events, because they are random, will be sometimes positive and sometimes negative, so tending to cancel each other out and disappear from the final waveform. This can be seen happening in the simulation shown in figure 4.5. In practice we use the computer to calculate an average from many samples, often over 500. Each sample consists of the EEG for up to 1 second from stimlus onset. We consider that the AEP so discovered represents the brain's typical response to a stimulus.

AEPs can be formed for visual, auditory, or tactile stimuli. Each produces a typical waveform, and examples are shown in figure 4.6. They are generally assessed by identifying the major **components** which are the peaks and troughs in the AEP, which are then translated into measurements of amplitude (size) and latency (time from onset of stimulus).

Particular features in the AEP have been identified and associated with specific mental processes. Experiments have been performed in which the

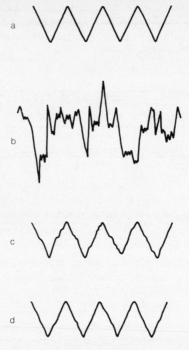

FIGURE 4.5   *Illustration of the principle of waveform averaging: (a) the underlying waveform; (b) with added random noise; (c) after averaging 32 samples of the noisy signal; (d) after averaging 512 samples of the noisy signal, showing that the waveform has been accurately extracted (From Beaumont, 1983)*

psychological demands of the experimental task are systematically varied. Concomitant changes in the AEP are inferred to reflect the differences in mental processes which follow from changing task demands. The earlier components, occurring in the first 150 msec from stimulus onset, represent the perception and identification of the stimulus. Subsequent components represent the analysis and decisions which the subject must undertake for the task which has to be performed with the stimulus. A particularly interesting component is seen after about 300 msec from stimulus onset, and this seems to reflect the mental elaboration of the stimulus (Lehmann and Callaway, 1979).

Sleep

The continuum of behavioural arousal varies not only between alertness and drowsiness or daydreaming, but also from wakefulness into sleep. Similarly, within sleep there is variation between lightly dozing and deep sound sleep. It is sometimes difficult to distinguish, physiologically, between different

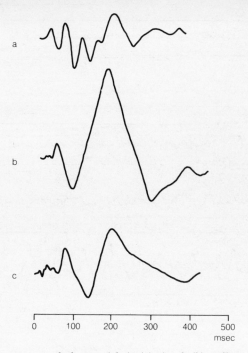

FIGURE 4.6 *Typical average evoked potentials in (a) visual, (b) auditory and (c) somatosensory modalities (positive up) (From Beaumont, 1983)*

levels of alertness while awake, but the change from wakefulness to sleep can be reliably detected.

The onset of sleep can be clearly observed in the EEG, and different levels of sleep can also be distinguished on the basis of changes in EEG activity. Sleep is generally divided into four stages according to the predominant EEG activity, with stage 1 being the lightest sleep, and stage 4 the deepest. Examples of EEG records from two individuals are shown in figure 4.7. During a normal night, sleep follows a typical cyclical pattern. Figure 4.8 shows the stages of sleep for one person through three different nights. Usually we fall quite rapidly into deep stage 4 sleep and then return up to lighter sleep, repeating this pattern about every 90 minutes through the night. You may have noticed that if, after waking naturally in the morning you go back to sleep and sleep on, it may well be over an hour before you wake again. Through the night the cycles become progressively less deep with more of stage 1 and 2 sleep.

At certain periods during the night, almost always during stage 1 sleep, rapid movements of the eyes can be seen. This is **D-sleep** or **REM** (rapid eye movement) or **paradoxical** sleep, sometimes also referred to as **active sleep**. This is to distinguish it from the sleep which occurs during the normal four stages which is known as **S-sleep**, or **passive** sleep. Sleep in stages 3 and 4 is

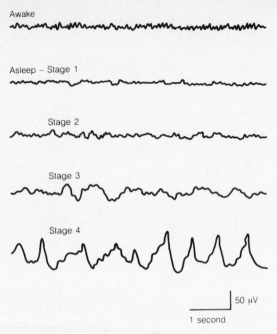

Awake

Asleep – Stage 1

Stage 2

Stage 3

Stage 4

50 μV

1 second

FIGURE 4.7 *The four stages of sleep as indicated by EEG activity. Note the increasing irregularity and large amplitude slow waves which appear in deeper sleep (From* Introduction to Psychology, *5th edition, by Ernest R. Hilgard, Richard C. Atkinson and Rita L. Atkinson, copyright © 1971 by Harcourt Brace Jovanovich, Inc. Reprinted by permission of the publisher)*

also referred to as **slow-wave sleep**. D-sleep also increases in amount as the night progresses (see figure 4.8). D-sleep is believed to be associated with dreaming, although there is continuing debate about the strength of this association. It is certainly the case that if sleeping subjects showing rapid eye movements are woken, they report that they were dreaming about 80 per cent of the time. This is less commonly the case when subjects are woken at other times during the night when no REM activity is occurring, and dreams are reported on only about 20 per cent of occasions. There may also be a difference in the quality of dreams reported on waking from D-sleep or S-sleep. Awakening from D-sleep is more likely to lead to reports of dreams in which there is an organized sequence of events with a 'story' to it; while dreams reported on awakening from other stages of sleep may consist only of isolated images. It may of course be that this distinction is merely an artifact of the ability to recall dreams. Awakening from S-sleep may result in the dream being forgotten before the person is sufficiently awake to report it, while waking from D-sleep may allow the ongoing dream to be remembered and then reported.

It seems that we 'need' to dream for a certain period each night. At least, if subjects are deprived of D-sleep (most simply by waking them every time

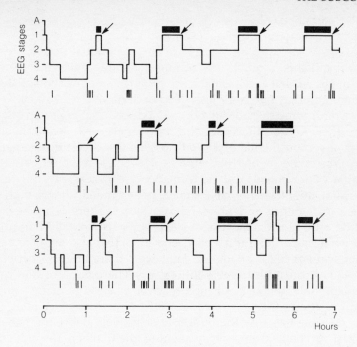

FIGURE 4.8   *The cycle of sleep through its four stages on three representative nights. The thick bars indicate the presence of rapid eye movements, and the vertical lines below show major body movements. The arrows indicate the end of each cycle. Note the irregularity of the cycles and the decreasing depth of cycles through the night (From Dement and Kleitman, 1957)*

they go into a period of REM), the amount of dreaming will increase on subsequent nights. Similarly, certain drugs reduce the amount of spontaneous dreaming activity that occurs. When patients stop taking the drug the amount of D-sleep increases above normal levels for a period before returning to normal. It is as if the lost dream-time has to be made up.

However, no one knows why we dream. Not many psychologists accept that there is any very deep significance in the content of dreams. Most commonly dreams seem to reflect odd events and information from the day reassembled in a rather mixed-up fashion. It may be that the brain is working out potential responses to an alternative turn of events, preparing for the worst. That may be why we sometimes have frightening or embarrassing experiences in dreams. On the other hand, it may be that there is a creative rearrangement of material from the day. It may be that the brain is rehearsing some of the material to allow learning processes to operate more effectively. However, it is difficult to research any of these hypotheses, because dreams are such purely subjective phenomena.

Similarly, we are not entirely sure why we sleep. It is true that restorative processes tend to occur while we are asleep, but this may not be the *reason* for sleep. It may just be that sleep is a convenient time for this to happen. Total sleep deprivation results in some changes which suggest structural alteration in certain parts of the brain (Horne, 1978). However, subjects totally deprived of sleep do not become ill. They just become extremely sleepy and difficult to keep awake. There is some limited decline in mental performance, but this is much less serious than was once thought. It has also been suggested that less dramatic but long-term deprivation of sleep, by regularly taking perhaps an hour less sleep each night than you 'need', may result in harmful effects. Without normal constraints people tend to sleep longer than they would otherwise, and individuals who sleep longer seem to be better at certain mental tasks and to be more cheerful, energetic and active than those who regularly sleep less. However, it would be wrong to conclude that better mood and performance are necessarily the result of longer sleep. It might be the case that a better mood allows both better performance and longer and more relaxed sleep. There is no persuasive evidence that mild but regular loss of sleep is psychologically harmful. It is true that if we miss part of our normal sleep, then that also tends to be made up on a subsequent night or nights. However, there are also people who seem, naturally, to need extremely little sleep. There are recorded cases of people sleeping only half an hour nightly, over a period of many years, and suffering no ill effects (Mayes, 1983).

It is also possible to study the effects of selectively depriving subjects of stage 4 sleep, or of D-sleep, by awakening them when the EEG record shows signs of the relevant activity. Loss of stage 4 sleep seems to produce little change in behaviour apart from sleepiness as a result of repeated wakening. However, on subsequent nights there will be an increase in stage 4 sleep. The evidence regarding loss of D-sleep is not so clear. It has not been conclusively shown that selective loss of D-sleep results in psychological ill effects. However, there is some evidence of subtle effects upon learning and memory following D-sleep deprivation in both animals and man. It is difficult to establish such effects because in the case of D-sleep, its deprivation tends to result in the appearance of aspects of D-sleep in other stages and it may be that some of the functions of D-sleep are transferred to those other stages. As with stage 4 sleep, loss of D-sleep results in a rebound upon subsequent nights.

There are also remarkable differences in the amount of sleep taken by different species of animal. Cows and sheep sleep very little, and some sea-going birds and aquatic animals hardly at all. Lions sleep a great deal. The differences seem to depend on ecological situation rather than on physiology. Animals which easily meet their biological needs are probably best tucked up somewhere warm and safe for the rest of the time instead of roaming about and expending energy. This may well be why most humans sleep for quite a lot of each day. It might simply be, in evolutionary terms, the safest way to spend our biologically 'free time' (Meddis, 1977).

Whatever its function, sleep is controlled by centres in the hypothalamus interacting with the ARAS and with structures in the brain stem. A particular structure, the **locus coeruleus**, seems to control D-sleep, and another structure in the pons may be responsible for inhibiting motor activity during dreaming – preventing us from acting out our dreams. All these structures are part of the general system which controls physiological arousal in the brain.

Altered states of awareness

Besides the normal continuum of sleep–wakefulness there are a number of states of special or **altered consciousness**. Some of these occur under the influence of drugs, medical and non-medical. Anaesthesia is a special case of altered consciousness. There are also 'out-of-the-body' experiences and those which some would regard as, perhaps, spiritual or paranormal. However, two particular states have been important to psychologists: hypnosis and meditation.

Hypnosis is unusual in that it is not associated with any clear physiological changes. However, there is no doubt that hypnotically induced states are real enough. Hypnotic analgesia, allowing subjects to undergo normally painful experiences without feeling pain, is a clear demonstration of this. Hypnosis can be induced by a variety of methods, often much simpler than the elaborate rigmarole of the stage hypnotist. Most people can be hypnotized, provided they are willing, although some are more easily put into a trance than others. The difference seems to be one of **suggestibility**, more suggestible subjects being more easily hypnotized. The hypnotic state once induced involves not only suggestibility, but also loss of volition (will) and control of attention, the adoption of unusual roles, and amnesia for events while hypnotized when released from the trance.

Although views differ, the most widely accepted view is that subjects understand what is involved in the role of 'being hypnotized' and are willing to take on that role. They accept giving up control over themselves, although their actions are not truly involuntary. This does not imply that hypnosis is a fake – patients *can* undergo surgery with only hypnosis as the anaesthetic. During such anaesthesia, however, there is apparently no suspension of normal physiological mechanisms as occurs with chemical anaesthesia. Hypnosis simply does not seem to constitute a fully physiological altered state of consciousness (Hilgard, 1985).

By contrast, clear physiological changes can be seen during **meditation**. Meditation may also be induced by a variety of techniques, but many involve bodily immobility and repetitive mental exercises. Sometimes the exercises are founded upon mantras, the private rehearsal of a single word or phrase. Some involve inward concentration on the 'stream of consciousness' and enhanced awareness of bodily sensations. Biofeedback (see p. 108) has been used to try to induce particular, and unusual states.

Most effective meditational practices induce changes in the EEG. The most typical change is an increase in alpha activity, which seems reasonable as the meditation involves deep relaxation and a de-focusing of attention away from the external world. Some studies have also found an increase in the slower theta activity in states of transcendental meditation ('TM'). This may indicate that a special state of the brain is being induced by these particular methods (West, 1982).

In association with meditation, Eastern yogis can also achieve quite remarkable feats of bodily control. Extraordinary reductions in metabolic activity (sometimes involving being 'buried alive' for lengthy periods), and control over heart rate and blood pressure have been carefully documented, although levitation has not been scientifically demonstrated. It may be that with long training and practice, such individuals can direct attention so effectively upon their internal physiological processes that direct control becomes possible.

How all this relates to our own subjective experience of the rich and constant running stream of consciousness remains a mystery. We each report a remarkable awareness of the mental and physical events of our own lives during our waking hours. Few significant advances have yet been made to help us understand where this awareness originates and why it seems that it is so special a feature of human life.

Motivation

Needs, drives and reward

Motivation is one of the central concepts of psychology. A given behaviour will not be seen unless the individual is motivated to perform the relevant actions. We can never know, for example, whether an animal has learned to perform some given task unless we can motivate the animal to attempt to perform it.

Motivation is ultimately based upon need and drives. **Needs** are purely *physiological*, and in their basic form imply a lack of something which is essential to continued existence. The needs for food and drink are the most obvious needs. If they cannot be met, the animal soon dies. Some other needs – sexual needs, the needs to explore and (in some species) to associate with others – are not quite such direct needs, but can be seen to be biologically necessary if the animal is to have a good chance of both surviving and reproducing.

Drives, however, are purely *psychological*, although they are related to physiological needs. The drive is what governs the behaviour which is directed to fulfilling the need. Hunger is the drive which meets the need for food, thirst which governs drinking, and so on. Although the drives are associated with the needs, they are not identical to the needs. A starving person has more and more need of food as time goes by, but hunger does not necessarily continue to increase. Hunger may have reached a peak beyond which it is not possible to become more hungry, physical weakness may modify the hunger, or other competing drives for water or to care for children may reduce the drive to obtain food.

In humans, **secondary drives** may be based upon the **primary drives**.

These are less clearly related to physiological needs. The drives to be successful, to be a good spouse, to earn money, or to be helpful to others are all largely learned. It seems, however, sensible to see them as based upon primary drives and so indirectly upon physiological needs. As children we learn to be obedient so that we will be loved and fed and cared for, and avoid punishment. As an adult, childhood obedience becomes social conformity and co-operation.

Linked with needs and drives are *rewards*. Anything which reduces a drive (and so meets a need) is rewarding. If you are hungry, food is rewarding and if you have a drive for social approval, praise will be rewarding. The mechanisms in the brain which register reward have a particular location.

In our discussion of the hypothalamus (see p. 6) it has already been pointed out that there are centres in the hypothalamus which control the onset and offset of behaviour such as eating and drinking. These must, in some way, be linked to the state of drives. We have also noted that stimulation of certain sites in the brain, in the region of the hypothalamus, is in itself rewarding. This dramatic discovery by Olds and Milner (1954) was that rats would stimulate themselves almost unceasingly if electrodes were placed in the limbic system, and particularly in the hypothalamus. A rat might press a lever to deliver the stimulation 2,000 times over 24 hours before taking a period of sleep and then starting to press again. Research eventually showed that the most effective site for electrical self-stimulation was in the **medial forebrain bundle** as it passes through the hypothamalus. This bundle of neurons connects the midbrain to higher structures and contains both ascending and descending fibres. This work supported the idea that the hypothalamus is central in the brain reward system. This view is known as the **hypothalamic drive model**.

More recent research has, however, concentrated on systems in this region of the brain which operate by the use of the neurotransmitters dopamine and noradrenaline (known together as **catecholamines**). It is relevant that these systems have a particularly high density of fibres in the hypothalmic region of the medial forebrain bundle. It has also been shown that these neurotransmitters are released from limbic structures during rewarding stimulation of the brain, and that drugs which interfere with the operation of these pathways also reduce the effectiveness of self-stimulation.

These systems have been traced to run from the brain stem via the midbrain and subcortical forebrain up to the cortex. They therefore provide an opportunity for cognitive events to be involved in motivation and reward. Expectations, and cognitive secondary drives, must presumably involve the operation of incentives at a cortical level, and these could have their effect through the neurotransmitter pathways, modifying the effects of the hypothalamus and associated limbic structures (Bolles, 1972).

Recent theories have therefore tended to argue that there are quite widespread influences, throughout the brain, which can regulate through particular neurotransmitter systems the operation of the fundamental mechanisms of drive and reward which are located in the region of the hypothalamus.

Hunger and thirst

Earlier views that hunger and thirst are simply controlled by 'on' and 'off' centres for eating and drinking in the hypothalamus have also been much modified by recent research. Eating, in particular, is an activity which is influenced by a wide variety of physiological mechanisms, as well as by habits and social influences.

In animals, a constant weight is generally maintained by varying the time between meals. If the animal succeeds in obtaining a large meal, it will wait longer before it feeds again. The size of the meal when it is taken, however, will not depend so much on the time since the previous meal as on how varied and tasty is the food. This suggests that different processes control starting and stopping eating. There may also be clues here as to why humans find it relatively hard to control their body weight: meals are usually taken at regular intervals without regard to the size of a previous meal, and the variety and palatability of food is very much greater than would be the case in a natural environment.

The business of obtaining nutrition can be divided into two phases. The first is an **absorptive** phase while nutrients are being absorbed through the intestine, and excess energy is being stored as fat. Insulin release stimulates uptake of glucose by the cells. This is followed by the second **fasting phase** after the gut has been emptied, in which energy is drawn from fatty tissue and from the liver. Adrenaline and certain hormones are released to maintain blood glucose levels and the liver converts glycogen into glucose. The metabolism of glucose is different in these two phases and is important in controlling satiety (feeling full) and hunger in turn.

The role of the hypothalamus seems to be to monitor glucose metabolism, and as a result to control the release of adrenaline rather than to control hunger itself (figure 4.9). Hunger seems to result from structures in the liver which are sensitive to glucose, and which then pass information back up to the brain. Feelings of hunger can be controlled by stimulating or inhibiting the function of these liver receptors (Novin et al., 1974).

There are also mechanisms, probably involving hormones, which monitor the level of fat reserves and provide long-term regulation. Much more short term are effects associated with the activity of eating. Starting to eat tasty food actually stimulates the appetite, although the tastiness of a particular food declines as progressively more is eaten. Feedback from food in the mouth, from distension of the stomach and from food entering the duodenum also tend to inhibit further eating and so provide regulation of meal size. The general level of arousal also has an effect on eating, so that when excited or emotionally aroused we are likely to take more food.

Thirst is rather better understood than hunger. Fluid deprivation has two effects upon the body: there is a fall in intracellular fluid (within cells), and also a fall in extracellular fluid volume, in the spaces around the cells. The first change is detected by receptors in the hypothalamus which are sensitive

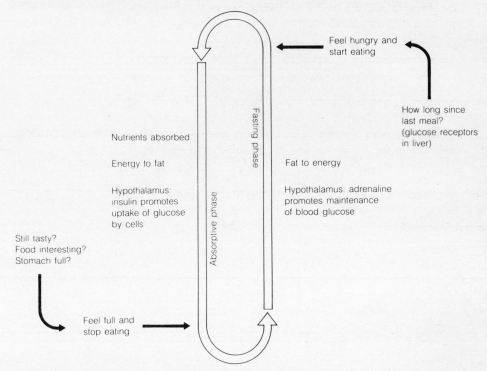

Feel hungry and start eating

How long since last meal? (glucose receptors in liver)

Fasting phase

Absorptive phase

Nutrients absorbed

Energy to fat

Fat to energy

Hypothalamus: insulin promotes uptake of glucose by cells

Hypothalamus: adrenaline promotes maintenance of blood glucose

Still tasty?
Food interesting?
Stomach full?

Feel full and stop eating

FIGURE 4.9 *A diagram of the principal mechanisms which govern eating*

to osmotic pressure (**osmoreceptors**). Osmotic pressure is used by the body to balance the concentration of substances inside and outside the cell membrane. As this is detected, the drive of thirst is increased. The change in extracellular pressure is detected by other pressure receptors (**baroreceptors**) in the walls of veins, and also by structures in the kidney which measure blood flow. Either of these seems to be able to initiate drinking (figure 4.10).

Besides stimulating thirst and generating drinking behaviour, these systems cause the release of antidiuretic hormone from the pituitary which causes the kidneys to concentrate the urine by reabsorbing some of the water contained in it. The kidney will also release a hormone which minimizes the fall in blood volume by constriction of the blood vessels. These mechanisms help to protect the body from the potentially serious consequences of rapid fluid loss.

Feedback from the mouth while drinking, or from a dry and parched mouth and throat, may also have an effect on thirst, but it is probably less important than the central mechanisms which are controlling the levels of fluid in the body.

Even though the mechanisms which control thirst are relatively well understood, it must be emphasized that drinking behaviour in humans is very complex. With both thirst and hunger, a variety of social and psychological factors influence the intake of drink and food. 'Drinking when we are not thirsty and making love all the year round . . . is all there is to

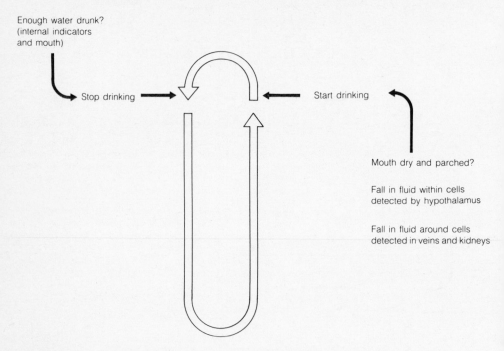

Enough water drunk?
(internal indicators
and mouth)

Stop drinking

Start drinking

Mouth dry and parched?

Fall in fluid within cells
detected by hypothalamus

Fall in fluid around cells
detected in veins and kidneys

FIGURE 4.10   *A diagram of the principal mechanisms which govern drinking*

distinguish us from other animals' (Beaumarchais). All of the physiological mechanisms are overlaid with a great deal of social and cultural learning, as well as cognitive expectations and desires. These can have a significant influence on the appetitive behaviours to be seen in humans.

Sexual behaviour

If social and cultural influences are important in determining hunger and thirst, they are even more important in controlling sexual behaviour. Although the hypothalamus is involved in sexual activity, as in eating and drinking, other factors also play a part.

One of these factors is the role of the sex hormones (see p. 25). Particularly in lower animals, the sex hormones are important in regulating sexual behaviour. Castrated male or female rats, for instance, cease to show any sexual behaviour. However, in humans the effects are not so straightforward. If an adult male loses his source of testosterone, sexual interest will only decline slowly over a lengthy period. Females who lose ovarian hormones seem to be little affected, although they may lose sexual interest after removal of the adrenal glands which are the source of androgens in females. Sex drive in humans is partly determined by the level of sex hormones circulating in the body, but only in interaction with the other factors determining sexual behaviour.

Neurotransmitters are a second factor influencing sexual behaviour. High levels of the neurotransmitter serotonin seem to depress sexual function in both males and females, and in females drugs which inhibit serotonin may increase sexual behaviour in the context of an appropriate hormonal state. Dopamine may also act in a similar way in females, and is more likely to increase sexual behaviour than to decrease it. These neurotransmitter systems are complex and the subject of active research. They are not yet well understood, but clearly have their influence by operating upon neural systems in the hypothalamus and elsewhere in the subcortex.

Within the hypothalamus there are areas which seem important in either promoting or depressing sexual behaviour, as there are for hunger and thirst. Lesions placed in a particular part of the hypothalamus may abolish sexual behaviour in male rats, despite normal levels of the sex hormones. The lesions may have their effect by reducing the influence of the hypothalamus upon other subcortical systems involved in reward and motivation. A different part of the hypothalamus seems important in controlling sexual behaviour in females. Lesions of this area may eliminate sexual activity, while electrical stimulation or stimulation through increased levels of hormones may increase sexual behaviour in rats.

However, in humans, external environmental factors are at least as important as internal physiological factors in initiating sexual behaviour. Sexually significant visual stimuli have an arousing effect in men and women, as does reading about sexual activity. Scents and perfumes also have some influence, perhaps because they contain pheromones which are naturally released chemical sexual attractants. Sex is a motivated behaviour like eating and drinking, and as with these activities, cognitive desires and expectations must partly determine the behaviour which is seen. Most of all, the emotional context is important in determining sexual behaviour as an activity involving two people who have complex feelings for each other beyond the simple fulfilment of sexual desires.

Learning

Learning is usually defined as a relatively permanent change in behaviour as a result of experience, rather than as a result of malnutrition or injury. It is a relatively stable tendency to react in some way, and the learning can only be demonstrated if an appropriate situation arises in which the reaction can be seen. Learning may be conscious, as when we come to know something we did not know before, but also occurs as we acquire habits or skills which may be outside awareness. In the broadest sense of the word, we are learning most of the time while we are awake.

Learning presumably involves a change in the functional organization of the brain. It is the great strength of the higher animals, and especially humans, that behaviour is not genetically pre-programmed but can be adaptive to the environment. In particular, simple forms of behaviour appropriate to an early stage in development can be replaced later by more sophisticated responses.

The concepts of motivation and reward are central to any theory of learning. Studies of animal learning clearly show that it is the behaviour which leads to drive reduction which is learned. If a behaviour is rewarded, and the drive therefore reduced, the behaviour is more likely to be repeated in a similar context. This is the whole basis of **operant conditioning** by which particular responses can be learned if they result in rewards being obtained. It may be demonstrated by rats pressing bars to obtain food (plate 4.2), monkeys solving problems to obtain peanuts, sea-lions balancing beach-balls to obtain fish, or humans pushing coins into 'fruit machines' to (occasionally) be rewarded by a jackpot.

Not only is reward important, but also the failure to obtain an expected reward. Unexpected **frustrative non-reward** is extremely powerful in abolishing certain behaviours, and may in certain circumstances be much more potent in reducing behaviour than punishment. The ability to discard unwanted behaviours is as important as the ability to acquire new ones.

However, it is also the case that learning occurs in a biological context. Animals in the laboratory will most easily learn responses that are similar to naturally adaptive responses (Breland and Breland, 1972). The natural foraging of rats involves exploratory behaviour quite similar to bar-pressing, and pecking is quite natural for pigeons. It is no accident that these have been the most studied behavioural responses. It would be very much more difficult to establish pecking in rats. The kind of information learned is also of adaptive relevance. Rats made ill by a substance with a distinctive taste will avoid similar tasting foodstuffs, but those made ill in a place with distinctive visual or auditory features will avoid similar locations (Garcia and Koelling, 1966).

Although the focus of this chapter is the subcortical forebrain, and so the relevant aspects of learning are those of motivation and reward, it is impossible to consider learning without realizing that it involves the whole brain. The level at which behavioural change occurs is at the level of individual synapses, and across all levels of the nervous system. Modification of the operation of reflexes in the spinal cord and of basic vital mechanisms in the brain stem can occur in response to repetitive and regular stimulation. Besides the operation of basic drives and reward mechanisms at subcortical levels, there is also a significant input from the cerebral cortex.

The cortex contributes a variety of aspects to human learning. The distinction between learning and memory is difficult to make and there is evidence that certain aspects of memory – in particular the way in which

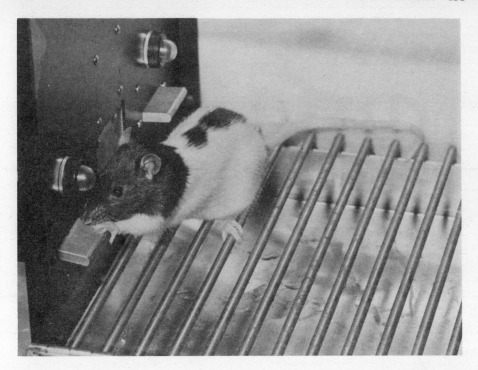

PLATE 4.2 *A laboratory rat in a 'Skinner box' presses a bar to obtain food reinforcement (Reproduced with permission of the University of Leicester)*

relatively long-term memories are laid down – are controlled by the cortex of the temporal lobe. Humans are also capable of being motivated by quite abstract conceptions of their own. Not only will they learn and subsequently perform for the satisfaction of simple pleasures, but also for beliefs and ideals (even if we might argue that these are ultimately based upon more fundamental basic drives).

Humans can also learn by instruction, and so by purely cognitive processes, without the need for practice or trial-and-error acquisition of behaviours which lead to rewards being obtained. We are even able to learn how to do things which we may never perform, simply by observation. You probably have a pretty good idea how to fire a rifle, how to milk a cow, or how to drive a stagecoach, although you may well not have done any of these. Even if you never do them, you will have learned something about the activities, although the learning remains **latent**.

The subcortical forebrain plays a central and highly significant role in generating and controlling a whole range of basic animal and human activities. It governs emotion, controls arousal and awareness, and provides the driving energy for basic learning through motivation. However, in all aspects of human behaviour, it operates in interaction with other levels in the nervous system. In particular it operates with reference to the cerebral cortex, and the intelligent cognitive functions which are organized there, modifying the expression of functions controlled at a subcortical level.

Further reading

A sound general text which covers many of the topics in this chapter is N. R. Carlson (1980), *Physiology of Behaviour* (2nd edn), Boston, Mass.: Allyn & Bacon. It is especially good on the basic subcortical systems as studied in research using animals. It is rather more advanced than Kalat (1984) (Further Reading, chapter 1), which would also be a useful text covering much of the same ground.

A. Gale and J. A. Edwards (eds) (1983), *Physiological Correlates of Human Behaviour*, London: Academic Press (in three volumes – vol. 1: *Basic Issues*, vol. 2: *Attention and Performance*, vol. 3: *Individual Differences and Psychopathology*) consists of collected reviews from specialist experts. It has particular strengths in psychophysiology as well as covering the standard topics of physiological psychology. A readable and stimulating survey of research on brain processes (both cortical and subcortical) involved in emotion is K. M. Heilman and P. Satz (eds) (1983), *Neuropsychology of Human Emotion*, New York: The Guilford Press. Undoubtedly the best guide to techniques is I. Martin and P. H. Venables (eds) (1980), *Techniques in Psychophysiology*, London: Wiley. It contains a wealth of practical and theoretical information about psychophysiological methodology. An alternative, less advanced and detailed text would be Hassett (1978) (Further Reading, chapter 1).

Discussion points

1 What autonomic emotional changes are clearly visible to other people? How important are they in communicating emotional states and in regulating social interaction?

2 What are the ethical considerations in deciding whether psychosurgery should be performed, and what specific factors should be taken into account in its use with an individual patient?

3 Is it possible to have a *scientific* study of the content of dreams?

4 Discuss any unusual states of consciousness you may have experienced: perhaps while very tired, after going without sleep, in connection with anaesthesia, or during an illness. What is different about the subjective experience, and how did it affect your attention to and perception of the external world?

5 Can complex human drives such as ambition or love be adequately explained in terms of more basic biological drives such as the need for food, for sex, or for care as an infant?

Practical exercises

1 Investigate the effect of time-of-day on a simple mental performance task. You might use mental arithmetic problems, as it would be easy to generate quite a large number of similar problems of equal difficulty. You might measure performance – the number correctly solved in a fixed period of time, perhaps – at two times in the day, either from one subject over a number of days or from a group of subjects tested on one or two days. The best times to contrast might be at the start of the morning and the start of the afternoon.

You could also measure body temperature if you wished, by using an ordinary clinical thermometer placed under the tongue (although do sterilize it between subjects!). Does body temperature relate in any way to better or poorer performance? You could even do an intensive study on yourself, with a large number of regular temperature readings, if you can find enough problems to solve and if you get someone else to read the thermometer and note down the reading so that you don't know what it is until the experiment is over.

2 Conduct an experiment to see if dreaming occurs more frequently later in the night. Use yourself as a subject, and an alarm clock to wake yourself at predetermined points during the night. It is probably best not to do it more than once or twice on any particular night – and don't disturb everyone else in the house! Have a pencil and paper by the bed so that you can immediately jot down information about any dreams you were having when woken – and then rapidly drop back to sleep. If REM sleep occurs more frequently later in the night, and dreams occur during REM sleep, you should find that dreaming is recorded more often after being woken later in the night.

3 Investigate whether variety of foodstuffs affects satiety. There are various ways in which this might be done, but an easy comparison is between the supply of a single foodstuff and the supply of a number of different but similar foodstuffs. The different foodstuffs should be equally filling and nourishing (and not likely to harm your subjects). You might use sweets of a similar kind but different colours and flavours. A good idea is to use custard, but to add artificial food colouring and flavouring (have you ever tried green custard?). Jelly already comes in conveniently different colours and flavours. Alternatively, you could use a pet, and offer proprietary food in different flavourings.

Your subjects need to be more or less equally hungry. Do not ask them to gorge themselves, but simply to eat until they 'feel full' or 'really don't fancy eating any more'. If you weigh the food before and after you will know how much has been consumed. Do subjects offered a variety eat more than those offered only a single foodstuff?

Box 4.1

Voluntary heart rate control as a function of individual differences in electrodermal lability

Some subjects are more successful than others in learning to control their heart rate. If voluntary heart rate control is to be a useful treatment technique in cases of anxiety and hypertension, it might be important to know who is able to gain voluntary control successfully. It would also be valuable to know why others fail. Katkin and Shapiro set out to discover whether lability of galvanic skin responses might be a related factor. Lability refers to how much spontaneous fluctuation is seen in autonomic activity in the skin. Individuals can be classified into *labile* subjects showing marked fluctuations, and *stabile* subjects showing few fluctuations. Katkin and Shapiro hypothesized that labile subjects would show greater control over heart rate because previous research had shown them to be perceptually more sensitive and to learn more rapidly under classical conditioning.

The subjects of their experiment were 24 male undergraduate students. They were seated in an easy chair in a quiet room. Skin conductance was measured from electrodes placed on the palms, and heart rate from standard ECG electrodes. Respiration was also recorded from a strain gauge attached to a tube placed around the chest. These physiological measures were continuously recorded on a polygraph and the information was then passed to a computer for storage and analysis.

In front of the subject were three instruments: a meter provided a continuous display of heart rate, a light bulb which flashed every time the heart rate was above a certain threshold, and a counter which indicated how many times the light had flashed. The subject was paid 2 cents for every count registered.

After receiving instructions, the subjects rested for five minutes. This was followed by 20 one-minute trials during which the subject was to increase heart rate as much as possible, but without muscular or respiratory manoeuvres. There were ten-second rest periods between trials. The threshold, above which the light would flash, was initially set as the average heart rate during the last two minutes of rest. If during the following trial the heart rate rose above this level, then the light flashed, one was added to the counter, and 2 cents were earned. After each trial, the threshold was reassessed. If less than 20% of beats in the previous trial were at a rate above threshold, the threshold was lowered by 2 beats per minute (bpm); if between 21 and 40%, then it was lowered by 1 bpm. If over 60% of beats were above threshold, then the threshold was raised by 1 bpm, and if above 80%, then by 2 bpm. The criterion of

Based on material in E. S. Katkin and D. Shapiro, *Psychophysiology*, 16 (1979), 402–4.

success was therefore steadily raised for those who succeeded, but allowed to fall for those who could not sustain a voluntary heart rate increase.

Subjects were assigned to labile or stabile groups on the basis of skin conductance fluctuations during the initial rest period. The eight subjects showing most fluctuations were designated the labile group, and the eight showing fewest fluctuations as the stabile group. The results of the middle eight subjects were discarded.

The design of the study, therefore, involves two criterion groups (labile and stabile subjects) selected on the basis of their spontaneous autonomic skin activity during rest. Membership of one of these two groups is the independent variable. The dependent variable is whether heart rate shows an increase or a decrease across the trials of the experiment. Other variables are held constant by the standard conditions of experimental testing (all subjects undergo the same procedure), by giving the subjects clear instructions (such as not to use breathing to produce an increase), and by randomization (randomly selecting subjects).

The mean heart rate during the last 2 minutes of the rest period was 75.2 (s.d. 10.7) bpm for the labiles and 79.8 (s.d. 11.95) bpm for the stabiles. There was no significant difference between these means (the F statistic the authors quote is equivalent to $t = 0.95$, df $= 14$). The subsequent mean changes, averaged over pairs of trials, calculated with reference to individual initial baselines, are shown in box figure 4.1.1. The divergence between the two groups is clear from the figure and is highly significant effect. Comparison of the mean heart rate of the two groups at the end of the experiment showed them to be significantly different (equivalent to $t = 2.84$, df $= 14$, $p < 0.02$).

The findings do not support the hypothesis put forward by Katkin and Shapiro. The opposite results were, in fact, obtained. The results clearly show that labile and stabile subjects differ in their ability to gain voluntary control of heart rate under the conditions of this experiment. The stabile subjects were able to increase heart rate, but the labile

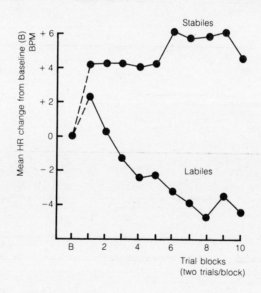

BOX FIGURE 4.1.1   *Mean heart rate change from baseline for labile and stabile subjects across ten trial blocks of two trials each*

subjects could not. The heart rate of labile subjects tended to decrease, rather than increase, across the trials of the experiment.

It is interesting to note that if the subjects had not been divided into two groups, and the mean results for all the subjects had simply been plotted, the resulting curve would have been a more or less horizontal line. We should probably have concluded that there was no evidence for subjects being able to gain voluntary control over heart rate.

The strength of the study is that it is carefully designed and well controlled. In so far as there are any weaknesses in the study, the value of the findings is limited by the decision to study attempts to increase heart rate but not attempts to decrease it. It might also be reasonable to wonder whether 20 one-minute periods was sufficient for voluntary control to be developed. The difference between the groups could be in the speed of learning rather than the absolute ability to gain control. There is also no adequate explanation for the actual pattern of results which was found and is not that which the experimenters predicted.

The experiment suggests that there are some subjects who can rapidly learn to control their heart rate, but that others cannot. It may be possible to use lability of skin activity to predict those who will learn rapidly. The experiment also emphasizes the need to consider individual differences in studies of biofeedback in learning to control autonomic responses.

Box 4.2

Relationship between circadian rhythm of body temperature and introversion–extraversion

Blake was interested to discover whether differences between 'morning' and 'evening' types on mental performance tasks were based upon underlying physiological rhythms. In this study he looked for an association between daily cycles of body temperature and personality.

Seventy-four young men were subjects, and their temperature was measured 20 times during the day on two days separated by one week. Temperature was taken by a standard clinical thermometer placed beneath the tongue. The readings were hourly from 7 a.m. to 11 p.m. and two-hourly through the night. The readings for each subject taken at the same time on the two days were averaged. The same pattern of tasks during the day was undertaken by all the subjects, and meals were taken at fixed times.

The subjects also completed the Heron Personality Inventory which gave a score for introversion–extraversion (I–E) on an 'unsociability' scale. Introversion–extraversion is a dimension of personality thought to have a physiological basis. Introverts tend to be quiet, unsociable, passive and careful, while extraverts are regarded as active, sociable, optimistic and outgoing. In this research a simple correlational model is being employed. The two variables of I–E and body temperature are correlated to discover if there is a significant relationship.

Correlation of the overall mean body temperature for each subject with their I–E score did not produce a significant correlation ($r = -0.04$). However, as box table 4.2.1 shows, some significant correlations emerged when temperatures at each time of measurement were taken separately. Positive correlations were obtained around 8 a.m. and negative correlations in the late evening between 11 p.m. and 1 a.m. As higher scores on I–E indicate greater introversion, this suggests that during the morning more introverted subjects had higher body temperatures, but that late at night more extraverted subjects had higher body temperatures.

This suggestion was examined further by selecting out a relatively extreme extraverted group (22 subjects with I–E scores less than 3) and a relatively extreme introverted group (25 subjects with I–E scores greater than 4). The pattern of body temperature through the day for the two groups is shown in box figure 4.2.1. There was no overall difference in mean body temperature between the groups ($t = 0.186$, df = 45). However, there is a difference in the pattern of temperature between the two

Based on material in M. J. F. Blake, *Nature*, 215 (1967), 896–7, used by permission. Copyright © 1967 Macmillan Magazines Ltd.

BOX TABLE 4.2.1   *Correlation coefficients (r) of body temperature and introversion rating at twenty times of the day (N = 74)*

Time	05.00	—	07.00	0.800	09.00	10.00
	−0.053	—	+0.133	+0.435‡	+0.163	+0.043
Time	11.00	12.00	13.00	14.00	15.00	16.00
	−0.013	−0.106	−0.054	−0.075	+0.006	−0.057
Time	17.00	18.00	19.00	20.00	21.00	22.00
	−0.042	+0.060	−0.016	−0.114	−0.239†	−0.167
Time	23.00	—	01.00	—	03.00	—
	−0.229*	—	−0.207*	—	−0.025	—

* p (one-tailed) < 0.05;   † p (one-tailed) < 0.025;   ‡ p (one-tailed) < 0.001.

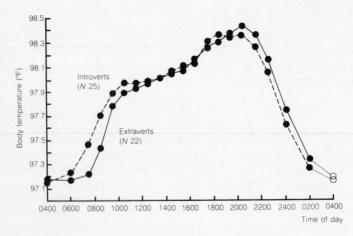

BOX FIGURE 4.2.1   *Body temperature rhythms of introverts and extraverts*

groups. It is clear from the graph that this difference lies in the introverts having higher body temperature during mid-morning, and lower body temperature during the later evening. The interpretation of the correlational data was therefore clarified.

Only a small relationship was demonstrated in this study, but it lends support to the idea that time-of-day performance differences between different personality types may have a physiological basis. However, it cannot be regarded as firm evidence for such an idea. Although the daily routine of the two groups was identical during the experiment, it might well be that individuals with different personalities adopt different life styles, and that their habitual activities lead to associated differences in the daily pattern of physiological changes. No correlational study can provide information about the direction of causal links. This study cannot tell us whether personality influences physiology, or physiology influences personality. (A critical discussion of this general question, and this particular experiment, can be found in W. P. Colquhoun (ed.) (1971), *Biological Rhythms and Human Performance*, London: Academic Press, ch. 3.) The strength of the experiment is that it is simple in its design so that the data, the analysis and the results are clear and easy to interpret. The weakness lies in its being a correlational study and the consequent difficulty of determining the theoretical significance of its findings.

References

Andreassi, J. L. 1980: *Psychophysiology: Human Behavior and Physiological Response*. New York: Oxford University Press.

Annett, M. 1985: *Left, Right, Hand and Brain: The Right Shift Theory*. Hillsdale, NJ: Lawrence Erlbaum.

Barlow, H. B., Blakemore, C. and Pettigrew, J. D. 1967: The neural mechanism of binocular depth discrimination. *Journal of Physiology*, 193, 327–42.

Beatty, J. 1983: Biofeedback in theory and practice. In A. Gale and J. A. Edwards (eds), *Physiological Correlates of Human Behaviour*, vol. 3, London: Academic Press, 233–46.

Beaumont, J. G. (ed.) 1982: *Divided Visual Field Studies of Cerebral Organisation*. London: Academic Press.

Beaumont, J. G. 1983: *Introduction to Neuropsychology*. Oxford: Blackwell Scientific.

Benson, D. F. and Barton, M. I. 1970: Disturbances in constructional ability. *Cortex*, 6, 19–46.

Binnie, C. D., Rowan, T. J. and Gutter, Th. 1982: *A Manual of Electroencephalographic Technology*. Cambridge: Cambridge University Press.

Bolles, R. C. 1972: Reinforcement, expectancy and learning. *Psychological Review*, 79, 394–409.

Breland, K. and Breland, M. 1972: The misbehavior of organisms. In M. E. P. Seligman and J. L. Hager (eds), *Biological Boundaries of Behavior*, New York: Appleton-Century-Crofts, 181–6.

Bunge, M. 1980: *The Mind–Body Problem*. Oxford: Pergamon Press.

Campion, J., Latto, R. and Smith, Y. M. 1983: Is blindsight an effect of scattered light, spared cortex and near threshold vision? *The Behavioral and Brain Sciences*, 6, 423–86.

Clare, A. 1980: *Psychiatry in Dissent*, 2nd edn. London: Tavistock Publications.

Code, C. and Muller, D. J. (eds) 1983: *Aphasia Therapy*. London: Edward Arnold.

Cohen, G. 1982: Theoretical interpretations of lateral asymmetries. In J. G. Beaumont (ed.), *Divided Visual Field Studies of Cerebral Organisation*, London: Academic Press 87–111.

Cox, T., Cox, S. and Thirlaway, M. 1983: The psychological and physiological response to stress. In A. Gale and J.A. Edwards (eds), *Physiological Correlates of Human Behaviour*, vol. 1, London: Academic Press, 255–76.

Dement, W. C. and Kleitman, N. 1957: *Electroencephalography and Clinical Neurophysiology*, 9, 673.

DeValois, R. L., Abramov, I. and Jacobs, G. H. 1966: Analysis of response patterns in LGN cells. *Journal of the Optical Society of America*, 56, 966–7.

Dimond, S. J. 1980: *Neuropsychology*. London: Butterworth.

Flynn, J. Vanegas, H., Foote, W. and Edwards, S. 1970: Neural mechanisms involved in a cat's attack on a rat. In R. F. Whalen, M. Thompson, M. Verzeano and N. Weinberger (eds), *The Neural Control of Behavior*, New York: Academic Press, 135–73.

Gale, A. and Edwards, J. A. (eds) 1983: *Physiological Correlates of Human Behaviour*, 3 vols. London: Academic Press.

Garcia, J. and Koelling, R. A. 1966: Relation of cue to consequence in avoidance learning. *Psychonomic Science*, 4, 123–4.

Gazzaniga, M. S. and LeDoux, J. E. 1978: *The Integrated Mind*. New York: Plenum Press.

Gibson, J. J. 1950: *The Perception of the Visual World*. New York: Houghton Mifflin.

Golden, C. J. and Vicente, P. J. (eds) 1983: *Foundations of Clinical Neuropsychology*. New York: Plenum Press.

Gregory, R. L. 1977: *Eye and Brain*, 3rd edn. London: World University Library.

Heilman, K. M. and Satz, P. (eds) 1983: *Neuropsychology of Human Emotion*. New York: The Guilford Press.

Hilgard, E. R. 1985: *Divided Consciousness: Multiple Controls in Human Thought and Action*. New York: Wiley.

Horne, J. A. 1978: A review of the biological effects of total sleep deprivation in man. *Biological Psychology*, 7, 55–102.

Horne, J. A. and Osterberg, O. 1977: Individual differences in human circadian rhythms. *Biological Psychology*, 5, 179–90.

Hubel, D. H. and Wiesel, T. N. 1962: Receptive fields, binocular interaction and functional architecture in the cat's visual cortex. *Journal of Physiology*, 160, 106–54.

Kertesz, A. 1979: *Aphasia and Associated Disorders*. New York: Grune and Stratton.

Kirk, U. (ed.) 1983: *Neuropsychology of Language, Reading and Spelling*. New York: Academic Press.

Lefrancois, G. R. 1980: *Psychology*. Belmont, Ca.: Wadsworth.

Lehmann, D. and Callaway, E. (eds) 1979: *Human Evoked Potentials: Applications and Problems*. New York: Plenum Press.

Liberman, A. M., Cooper, F., Shankweiler, D. and Studdert-Kennedy, M. 1967: Perception of the speech code. *Psychological Review*, 74, 431–59.

Loftus, E. F., Miller, D. G. and Burns, H. J. 1978: Semantic integration of verbal information into a visual memory. *Journal of Experimental Psychology: Human Learning and Memory*, 4, 19–31.

Luria, A. R. 1973: *The Working Brain*. London: Penguin.

Lykken, D. T. 1983: Polygraphic interrogation: the applied psychophysiologist. In A. Gale and J. A. Edwards (eds), *Physiological Correlates of Human Behaviour*, vol. 1, London: Academic Press, 241–54.

Marks, M. and Folkard, S. 1984: Diurnal rhythms in cognitive performance. In J. Nicholson and H. Beloff (eds), *Psychology Survey 5*, Leicester: British Psychological Society, 63–94.

Marks, W. B., Dobelle, W. H. and MacNichol, E. F. 1964: Visual pigments of single primate cones. *Science*, 143, 1181–3.

Masterson, R. B. 1974: Adaptation for sound localization in the ear and brainstem of mammals. *Proceedings of the Federation of American Societies for Experimental Biology*, 33, 1904–10.

Mayes, A. (ed.) 1983: *Sleep Mechanisms and Functions in Humans and Animals*. New York: Van Nostrand Reinhold.

Meddis, R. 1977: *The Sleep Instinct*. London: Routledge and Kegan Paul.

Miller, E. 1984: *Recovery and Management of Neuropsychological Impairments*. Chichester: John Wiley.

Munn, N. L. 1966: *Psychology*. Boston: Houghton Mifflin.

Nauta, W. J. H. and Feirtag, M. 1979: The Organization of the Brain. *Scientific American*, September 1979.

Novin, D., Sanderson, J. B. and VanderWeele, D. A. 1974: The effect of isotonic glucose on eating as a function of feeding and infusion site. *Physiology and Behavior*, 13, 3–7.

Oakley, D. A. and Plotkin, H. C. 1979: *Brain, Behaviour and Evolution*. London: Methuen.

Olds, J. and Milner, P. 1954: Positive reinforcement produced by electrical stimulation of septal area and other regions of rat brain. *Journal of Comparative and Physiological Psychology*, 47, 419–27.

Penfield, W. 1975: *The Mystery of the Mind*. Princeton, NJ: Princeton University Press.

Pincus, J. H. and Tucker, G. J. 1978: *Behavioural Neurology*, 2nd edn. Oxford: Oxford University Press.

Pirozzolo, F. J. and Wittrock, M. C. (eds) 1981: *Neuropsychological and Cognitive Processes in Reading*. New York: Academic Press.

Pryse-Phillips, W. 1969: *Epilepsy*. Bristol: John Wright and Son Ltd.

Robinson, J. O. 1972: *The Psychology of Visual Illusion*. London: Hutchinson.

Roederer, J. G. 1975: *Introduction to the Physics and Psychophysics of Music*. Berlin: Springer-Verlag.

Rolls, E. T. 1979: Effects of electrical stimulation of the brain on behaviour. In K. Connolly (ed.), *Psychology Survey* no. 2, London: George Allen and Unwin, 151–69.

Rushton, D. N. and Brindley, G. S. 1977: Short- and long-term stability of cortical electrical phosphenes. In F. C. Rose (ed.), *Physiological Aspects of Clinical Neurology*, Oxford: Blackwell Scientific.

Satz, P. 1979: A test of some models of hemispheric speech organisation in the left- and right-handed. *Science*, 203, 1131–3.

Schachter, S. and Singer, J. S. 1962: Cognitive, social and physiological determinants of emotional state. *Psychological Review*, 69, 379–99.

Silverstone, T. and Turner, P. 1982: *Drug Treatment in Psychiatry*, 3rd edn. London: Routledge and Kegan Paul.

Singleton, C. H. 1978: Sex differences. In B. M. Foss (ed.), *Psychology Survey* no. 1, London: George Allen and Unwin, 116–30.

Springer, S. P. 1979: Speech perception and the biology of language. In M. S. Gazzaniga (ed.), *Handbook of Behavioral Neurobiology*, vol. 2: *Neuropsychology*, New York: Plenum Press, 153–77.

Springer, S. P. and Deutsch, G. 1985: *Left Brain, Right Brain*, 2nd edn. San Francisco: W. H. Freeman.

Taylor, A., Sluckin, W. S., Davies, D. R., Reason, J. T., Thomson, R. and Colman, A. M. 1982: *Introducing Psychology*. London: Penguin.

Teuber, H.-L. 1964: The riddle of the frontal lobes in man. In J. M. Warren and K. Akert (eds), *The Frontal Granular Cortex and Behavior*, New York: McGraw-Hill, 410–44.

Treisman, A. M., Squire, R. and Green, J. 1974: Semantic processing in dichotic listening? A replication. *Memory and Cognition*, 2, 641–6.

Uttal, W. R. 1973: *The Psychobiology of Sensory Coding*. New York: Harper.

Valenstein, E. S. (ed.) 1980: *The Psychosurgery Debate: Scientific, Legal and Ethical Perspectives*. San Francisco: W. H. Freeman.

Van Toller, C. 1983: Biochemistry of the nervous system. In A. Gale and J. A. Edwards (eds), *Physiological Correlates of Human Behaviour*, vol. 1, London: Academic Press, 79–104.

von Békésy, G. 1960: *Experiments in Hearing*. New York: McGraw-Hill.

Vowles, D. M. 1980: Hormones and sexual behaviour. In M. Jeeves (ed.), *Psychology Survey* no. 3, London: George Allen and Unwin, 132–45.

Walsh, K. W. 1978: *Neuropsychology: A Clinical Approach*. Edinburgh: Churchill-Livingstone.

Warrington, E. K. and Pratt, R. T. C. 1981: The significance of laterality effects. *Journal of Neurology, Neurosurgery and Psychiatry*, 44, 193–6.

Warwick Evans, L. A. 1983: Psychosomatic disorders: theories and evidence. In A. Gale and J. A. Edwards (eds), *Physiological Correlates of Human Behaviour*, vol. 3, London: Academic Press, 170–86.

Weinstein, E. A. and Friedland, R. P. (eds) 1977: *Hemi-Inattention and Hemisphere Specialization. Advances in Neurology*, vol. 18. New York: Raven Press.

Wenger, M. A. 1966: Studies of autonomic balance: A summary. *Psychophysiology*, 2, 173–86.

West, M. 1982: Meditation and self-awareness: Physiological and phenomenological approaches. In G. Underwood (ed.), *Aspects of Consciousness*, vol. 3, London: Academic Press, 191–234.

Wiederholt, W. C. (ed.) 1982: *Neurology for Non-neurologists*. New York: Academic Press.

Young, A. W. (ed.) 1983: *Functions of the Right Cerebral Hemisphere*. New York: Academic Press.

Name Index

Subject Index